ADAM W. CLIFTON

I WILL FOLLOW YOU

PHOTOGRAPHS

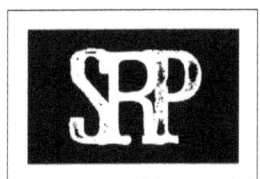

SIBLING RIVALRY PRESS
LITTLE ROCK · ARKANSAS
SIBLINGRIVALRYPRESS.COM

I Will Follow You
Copyright © 2015 by Adam W. Clifton

Cover design by Sibling Rivalry Press

All rights reserved. No part of this book may be reproduced or republished without written consent from the publisher, except by reviewers who may quote brief excerpts in connection with a review in a newspaper, magazine, or electronic publication; nor may any part of this book be reproduced, stored in a retrieval system, or transmitted in any form, or by any means be recorded without written consent of the publisher.

Sibling Rivalry Press, LLC
PO Box 26147
Little Rock, AR 72221

info@siblingrivalrypress.com

www.siblingrivalrypress.com

ISBN: 978-1-943977-00-0

First Sibling Rivalry Press Edition, October 2015

I
WILL
FOLLOW
YOU

FOR
October 3, 2013

SOMETIMES I ALLOW MYSELF TO THINK OF the city and my time there. He and I walking, I'd catch myself falling back to snap a photo, always of him, then jogging boyishly to catch up. He never waited. He was too in awe of the place and, even as everything everywhere was cast in January's cold, gray sunlight, I couldn't blame him. It was beautiful and seeing him there was warming. The back of his head a red beacon against the stony evening light, I followed, pulled by the ever-tightening cords between our chests, the ones that braided themselves while we slept and wove beautiful patterns when we kissed. I suppose love was happening to us. It was accumulating with every step, filling us up with each glance and gesture, and I could feel the weight of it in the way he turned toward me. *Hurry up*, he'd grin.

Would if I could, I'd have kept those walks and made them last forever. Maybe if you follow the sidewalk long enough the sun will never set and you'll never have to say *goodnight*, or *goodbye*, or *see you next time*. Maybe you start to think you've already made it to where you're supposed to be.

Sometimes I allow myself to think of the city and my time there. *I will follow you*, I determined silently, tailing closely behind. He led the way through the streets, every turn and crossing governed by the tilt of his head and the tug in my chest.

IT WASN'T UNTIL LATER, BACK AT HOME, that I began to see what I'd been missing on those walks with him. When the film was developed I was left with images of the back of my man's head, pictures of him turned away from me, face searching the streets, the sky, looking out and ahead, but never aimed at me. *What was he looking for? What was he thinking?* These images were a portrait of our time together. There was me out of view, but always watching, attentive, and there was him, turned away, not opening up, not letting me in on what was going on behind those deep blue eyes, hidden from me by the angle of his head, or that sweep of red fringe. I'd resolved to follow him and follow I would, but suddenly I found myself questioning where we were headed, and why.

There is a special relationship that a man has with himself, an intimate place within which no other is allowed. It is an empty room, a warm beer, a mess on the sheets. It's where thoughts purr and silence gains weight. It's the place where you decide whether to lay with him and spend the morning sticky, or to rise and shine and clean yourself up. There are private things there, secrets and qualms. This is not a fault. It's a fact, for all of us. No matter how open and honest we are, no matter how affectionate or sexual, our friends, partners, loved ones, can never really get how we are with ourselves when we're alone, when no one's around.

It became a kind of hurtful puzzle, a game for me, to find him in these places. I'd wait and watch to catch the distance on his face over coffee, or the way he'd sit at the edge of the bed some nights, elbows on knees, facing the wall. It was in the way he set his hands in his lap on the train and in the way he giggled to himself while reading the paper. It was the way he turned his head to the sky and sighed and jammed his hands into his coat pockets when we both noticed a couple, arm in arm, a few yards ahead of us one afternoon while walking along Cheapside. One hopeful look from me, a desperate-to-do-that-too smile. He had touched me more deeply than any man ever had, quite literally, but it felt as if I wasn't allowed to think those things. I knew but would have never admitted that I didn't stand a chance. In the case of him I was meant to follow, I think, to worship even, to stand behind and wonder at the big of him.

NOW I SIT ALONE, WORKING, WRITING, compiling these images in hopes that I've related what I've done my best to capture. In retrospect it's hard to excuse what I've done here. I spent a year photographing upwards of fifty men for this collection and when I'd finished, and taken a long, hard look at what I'd created, I found that I was still taking *his* picture. I was still following him through the city, along darkened hallways, across sunlit bedrooms and rain-slick rooftops. We don't take those walks anymore, he and I. That's over. But I'd be lying if I said that these portraits weren't entirely him.

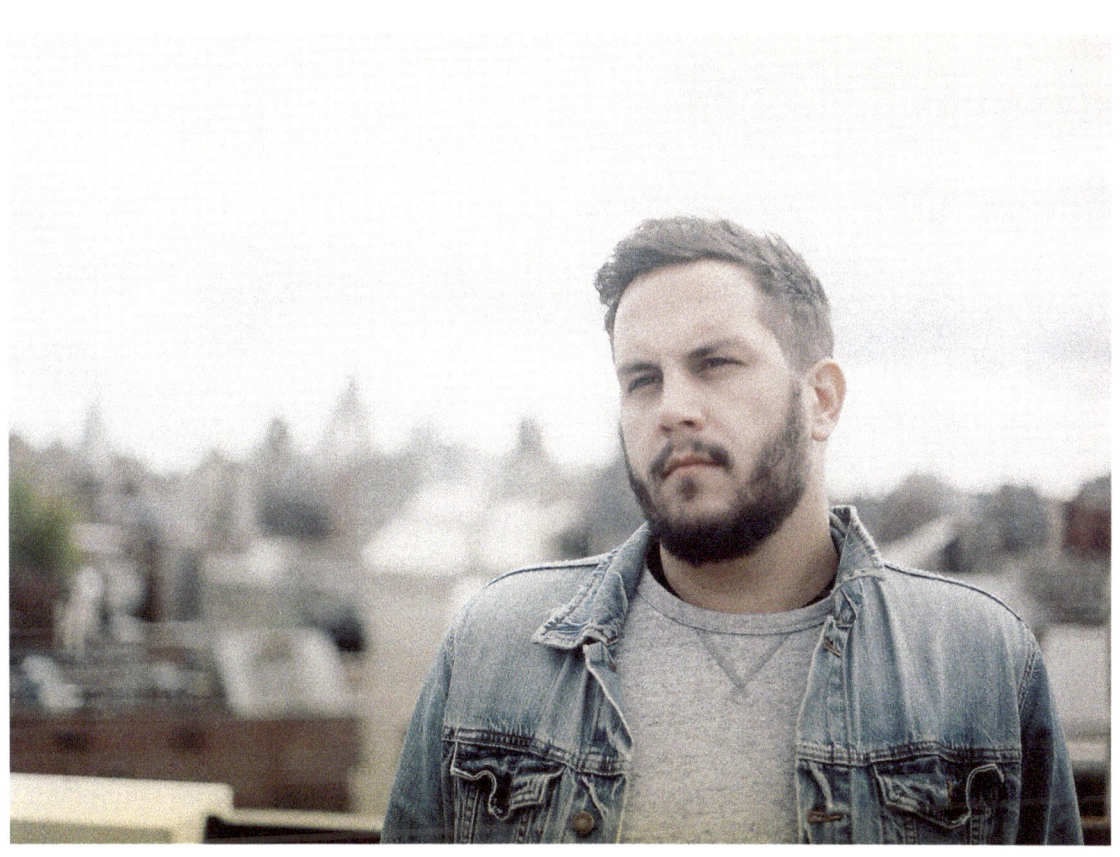

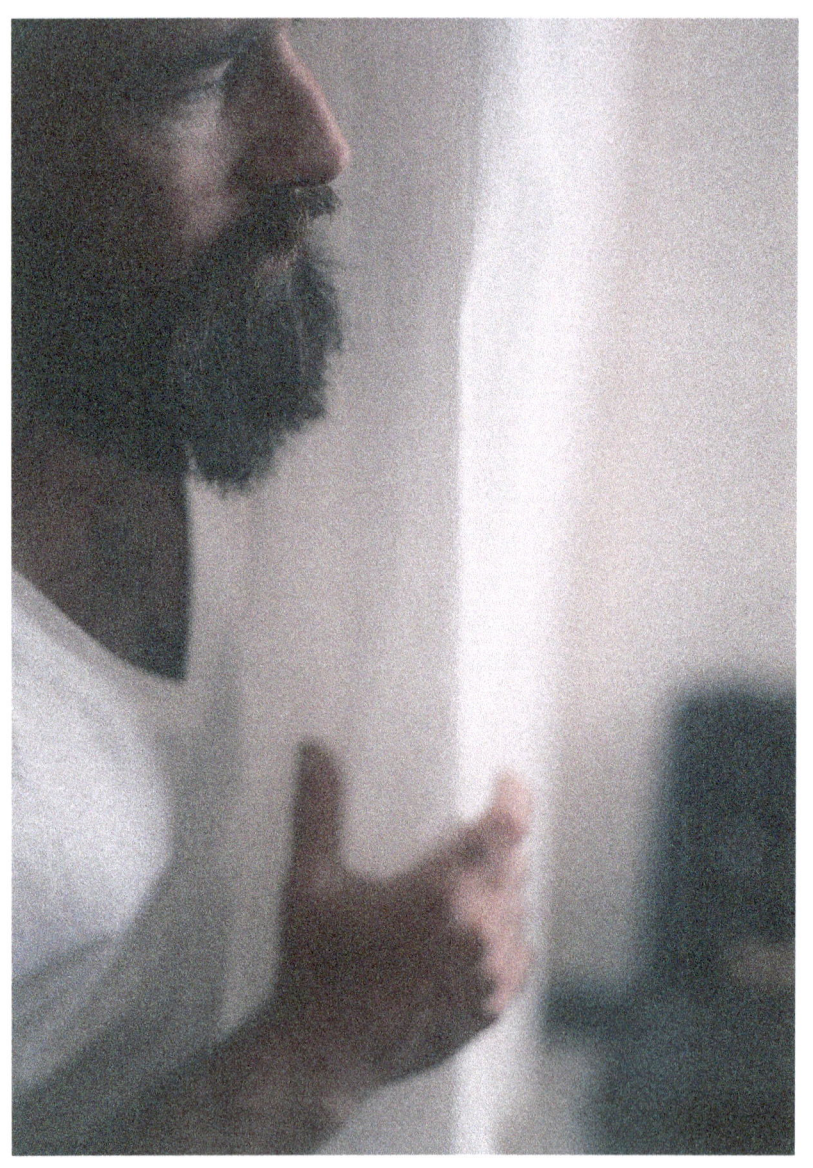

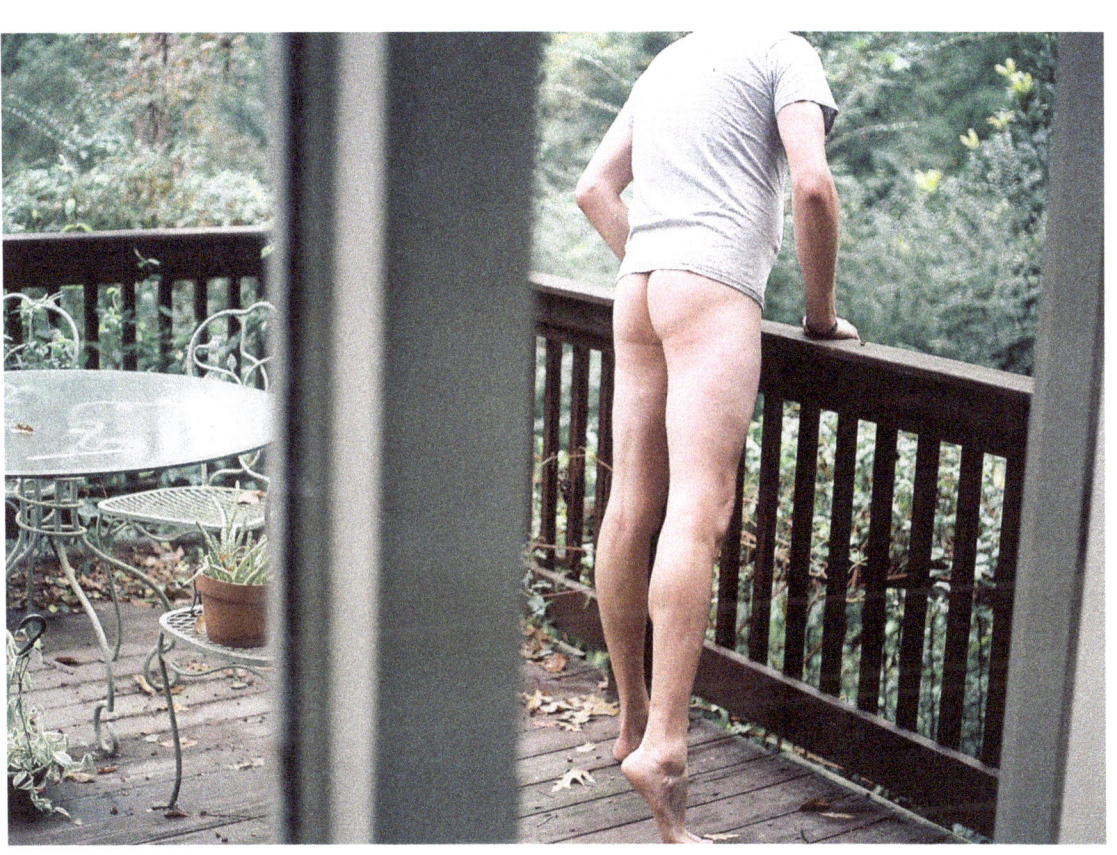

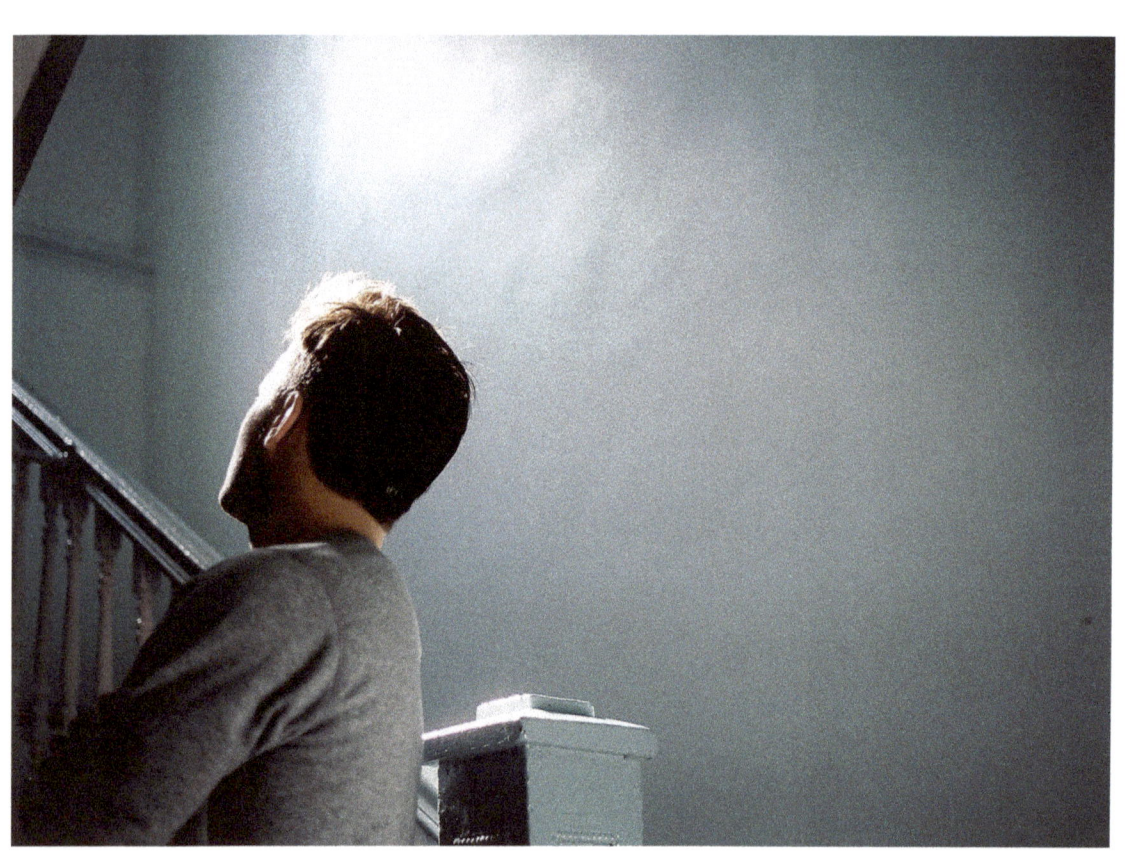

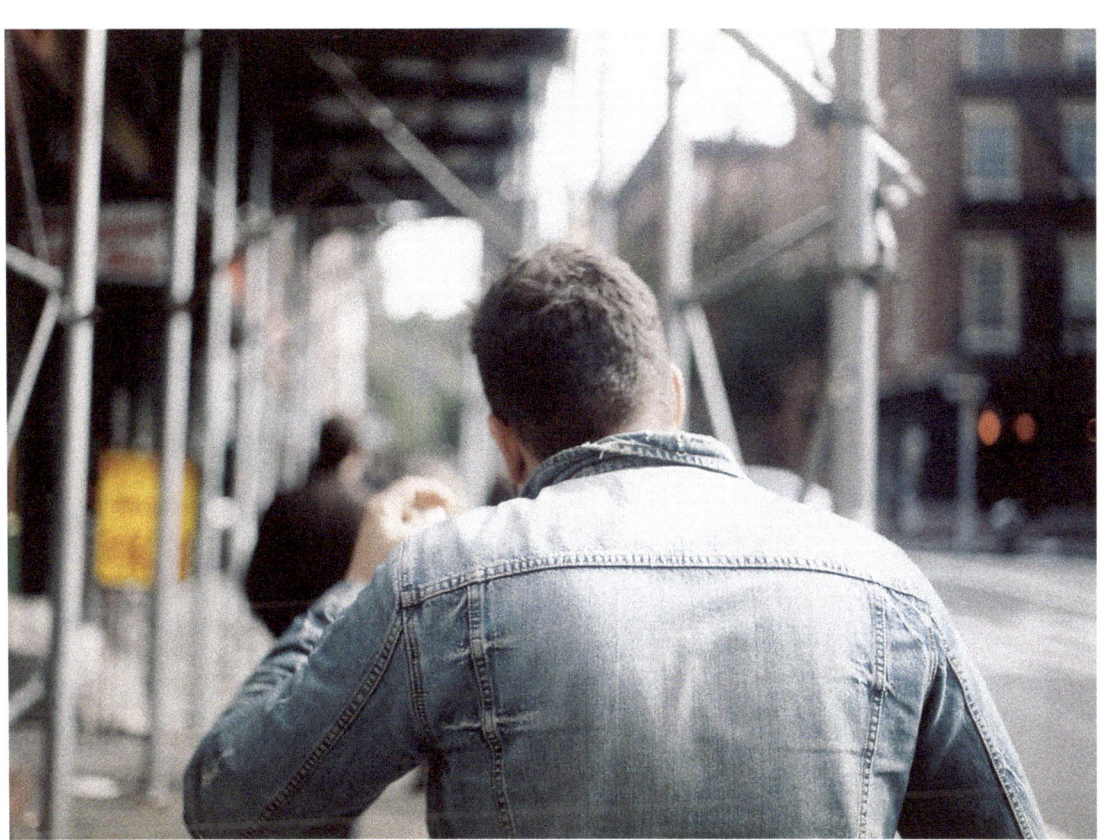

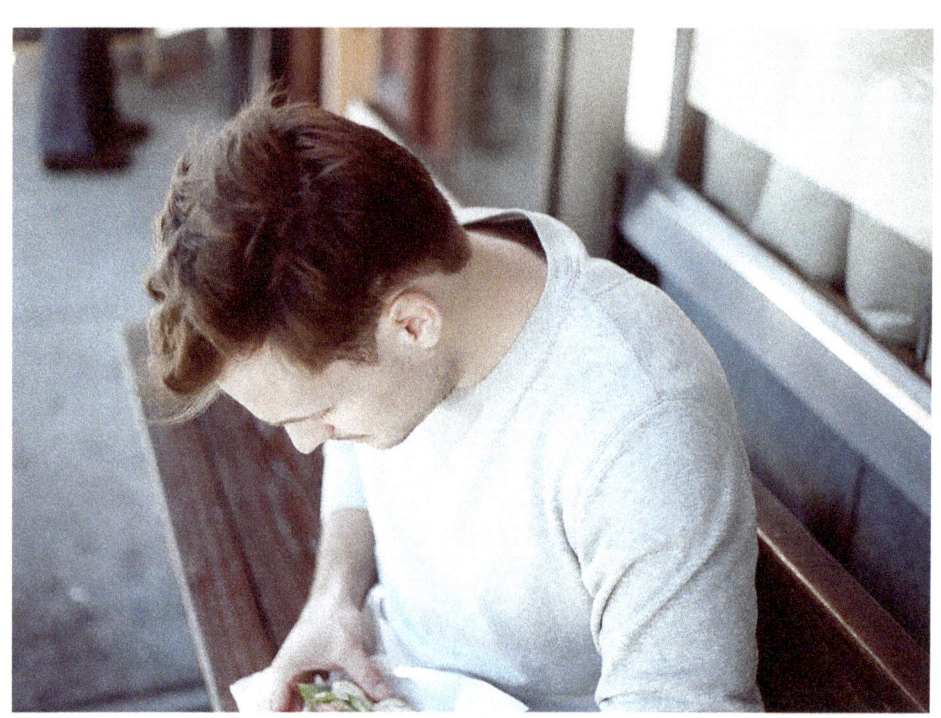

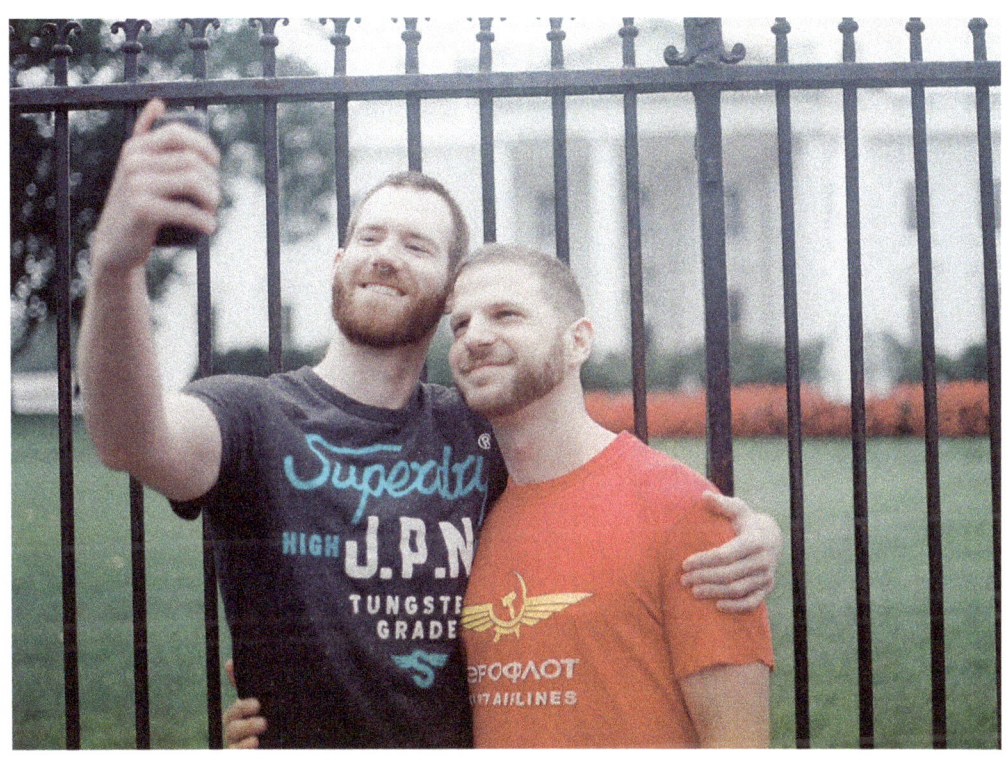

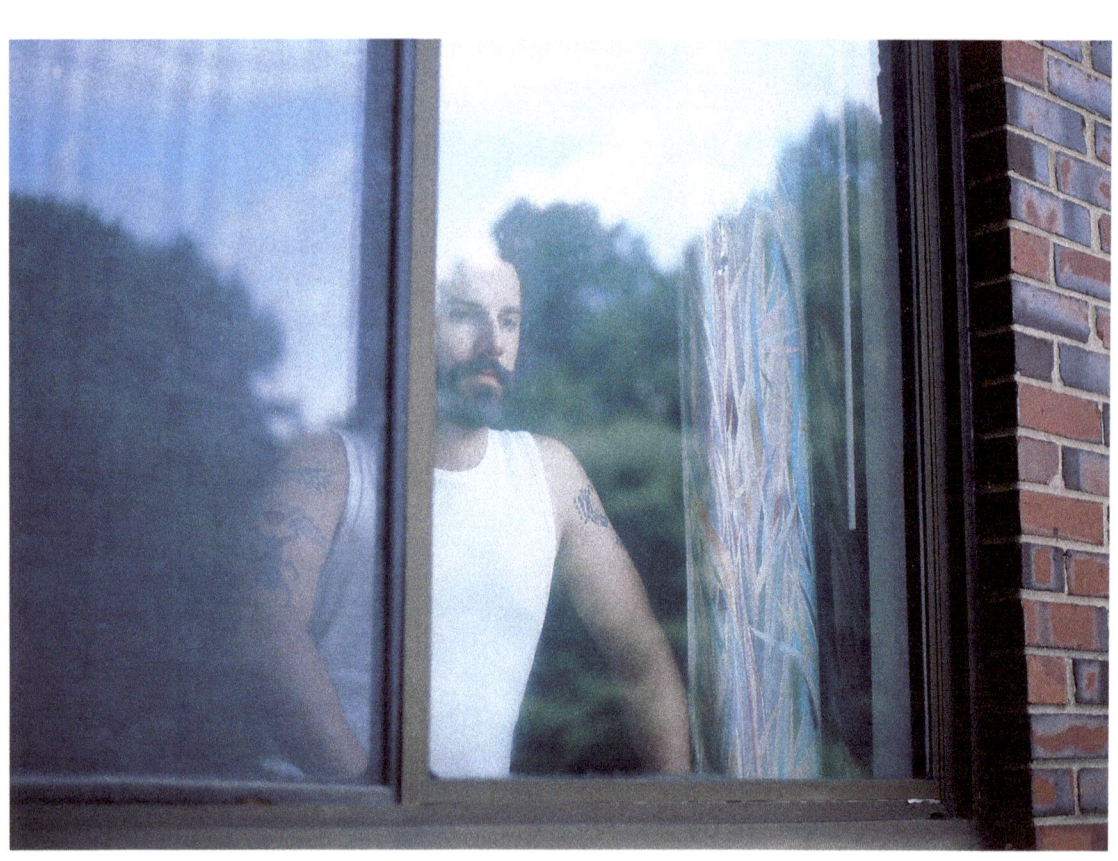

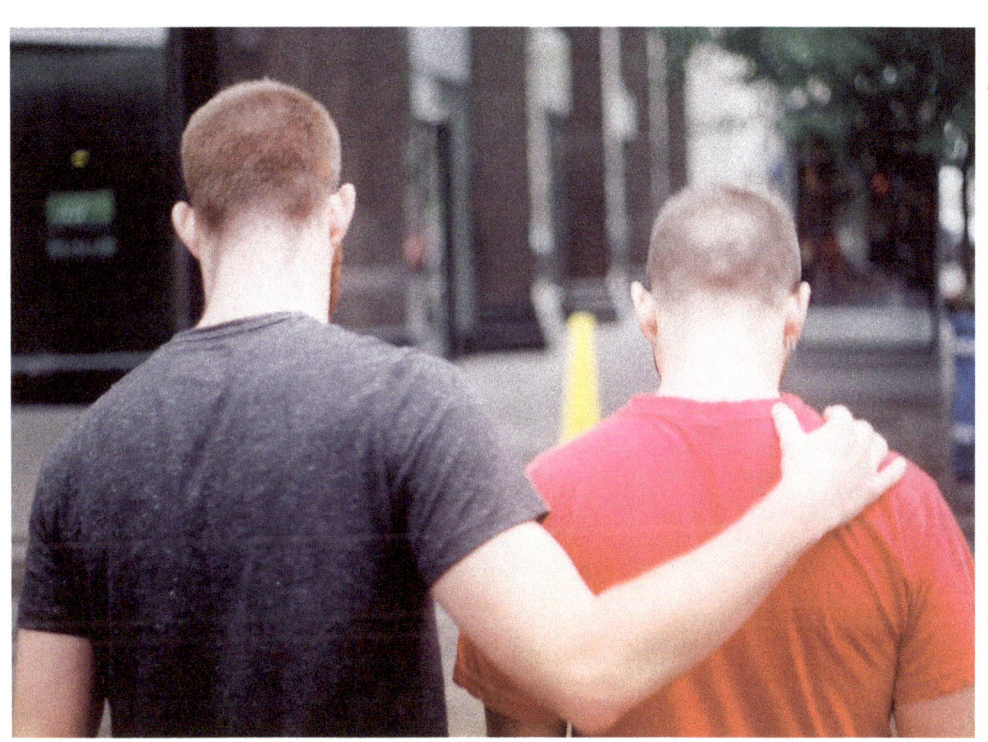

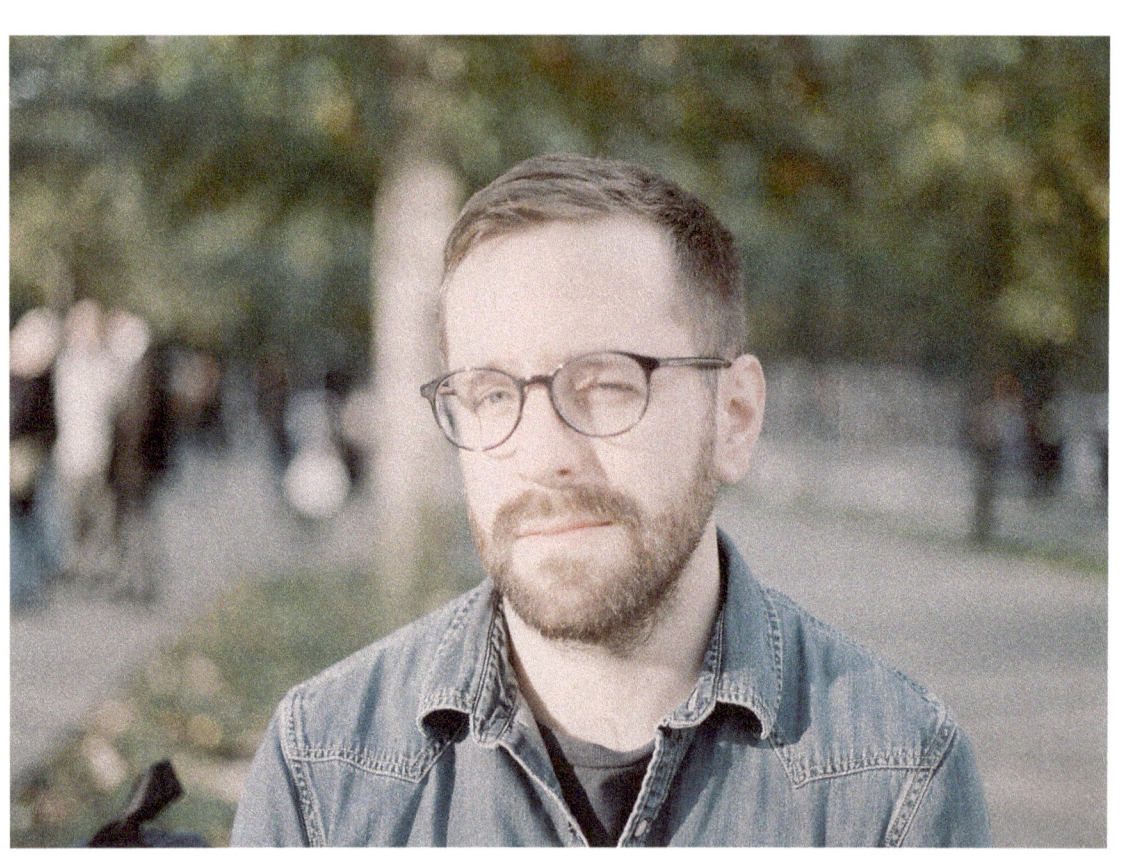

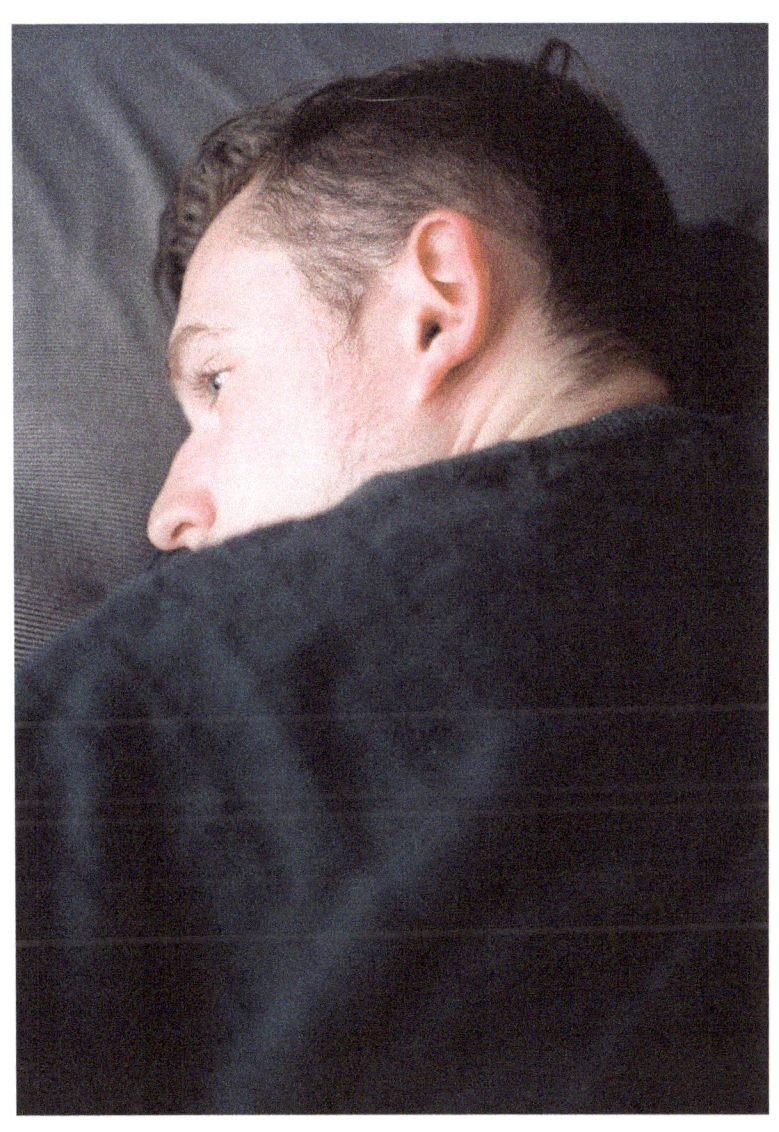

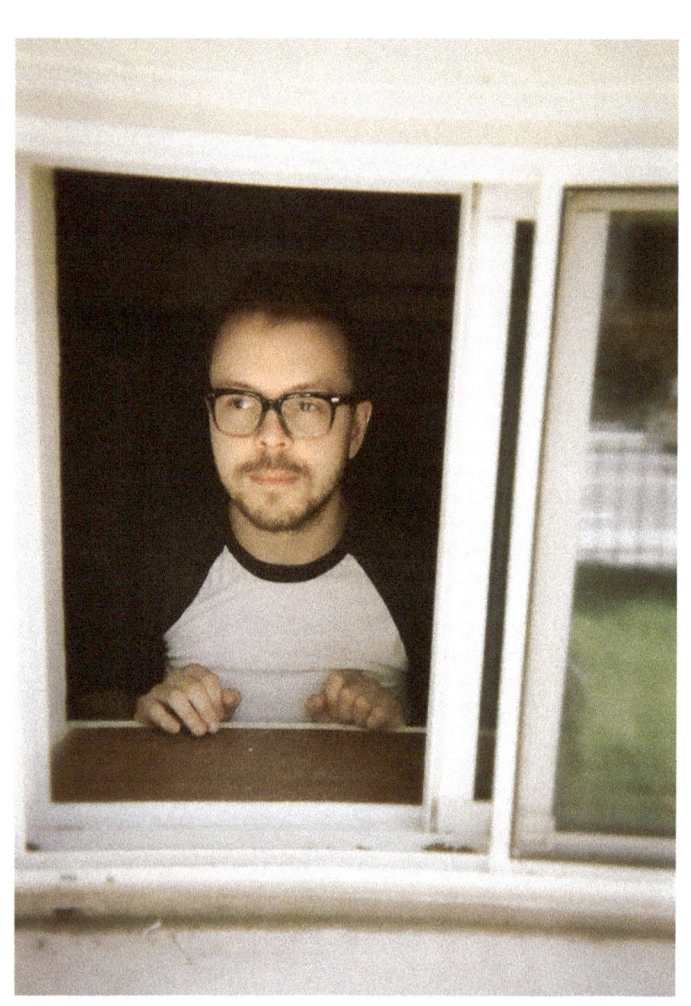

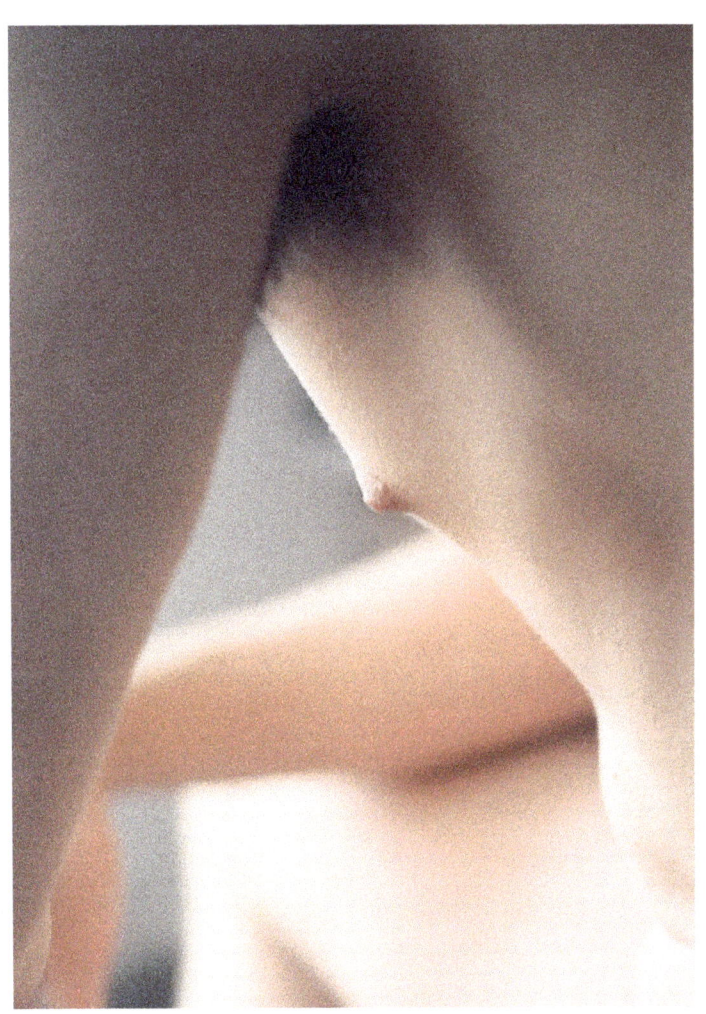

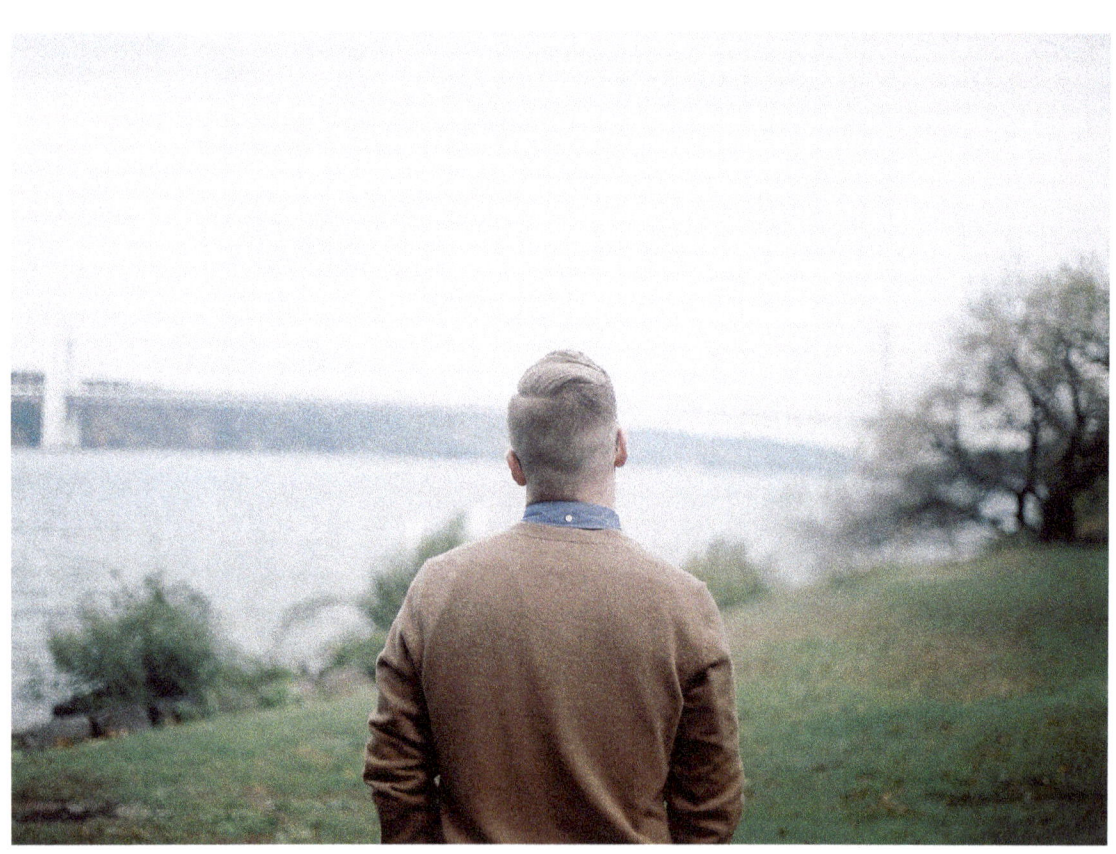

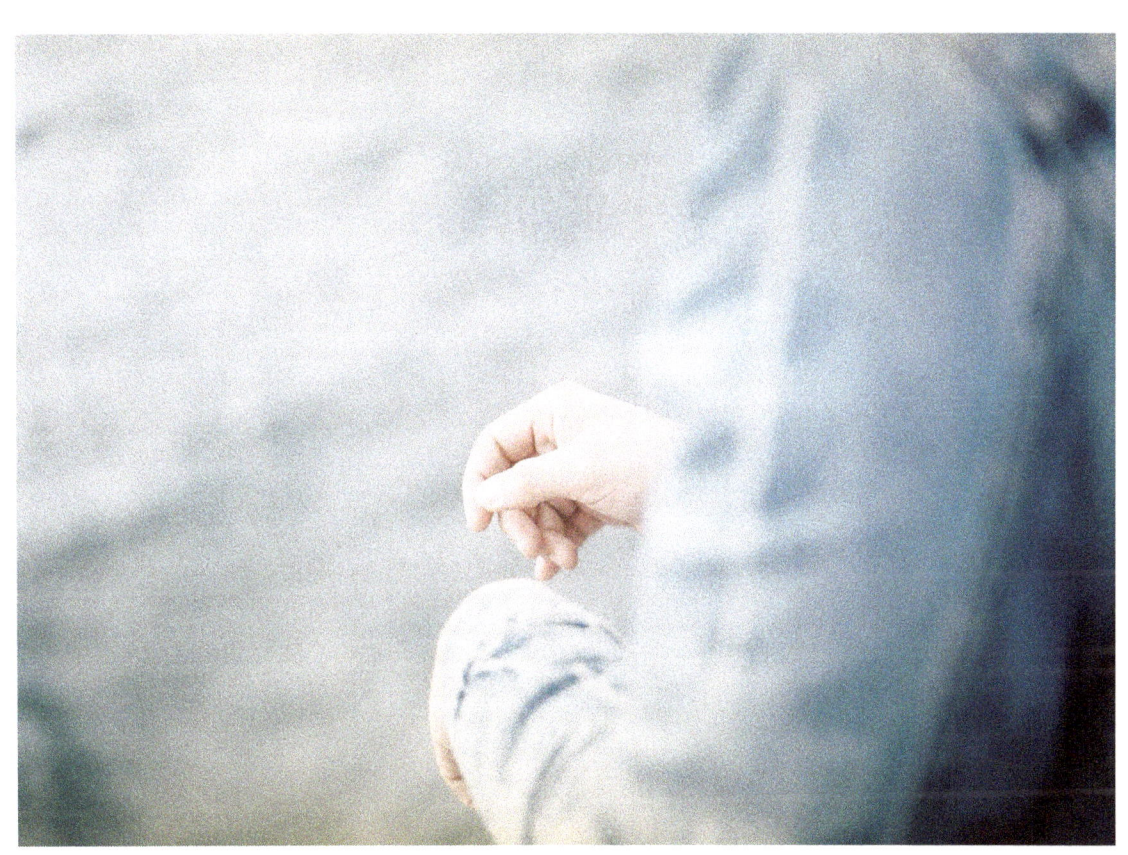

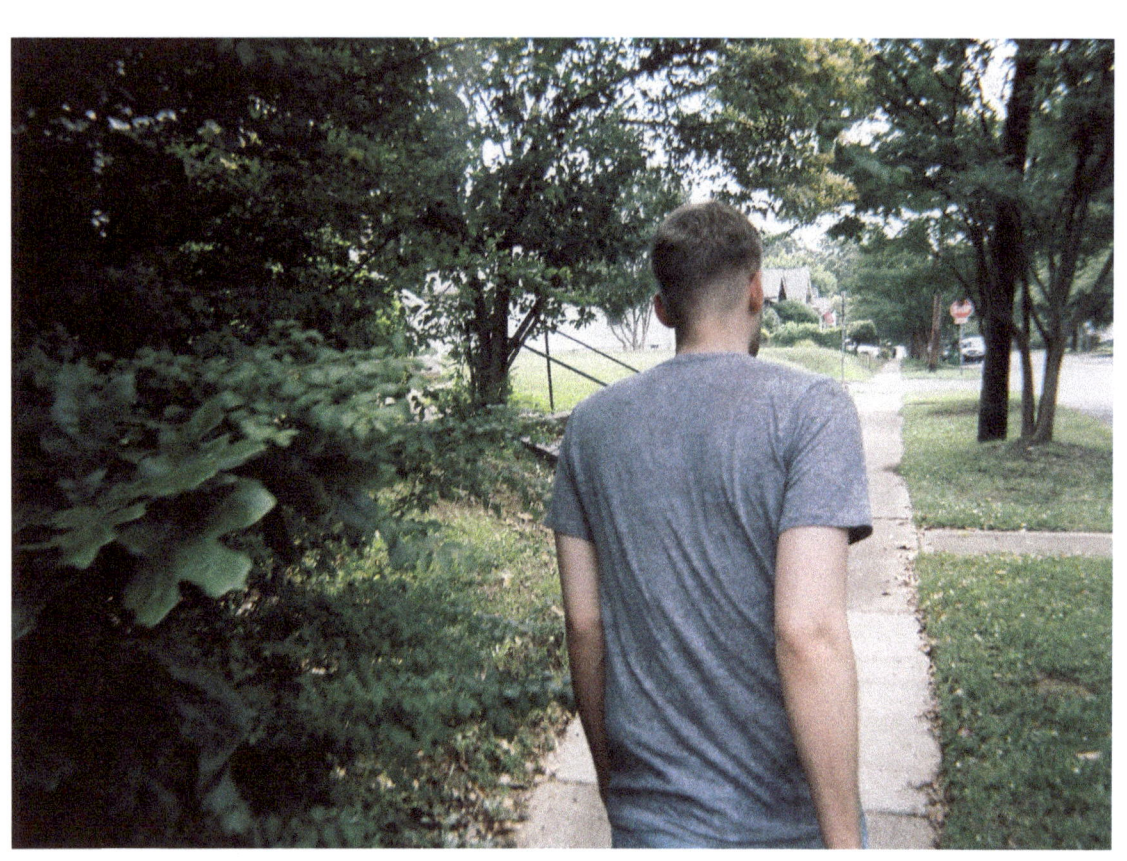

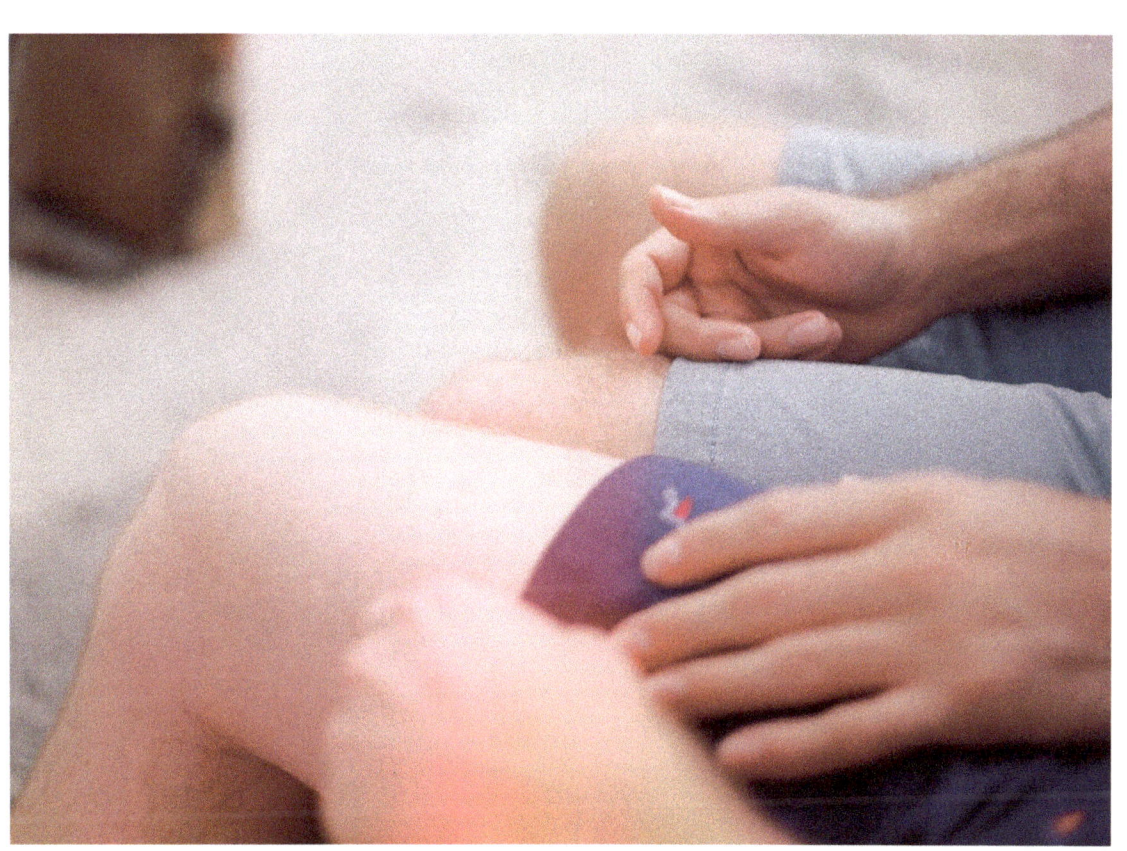

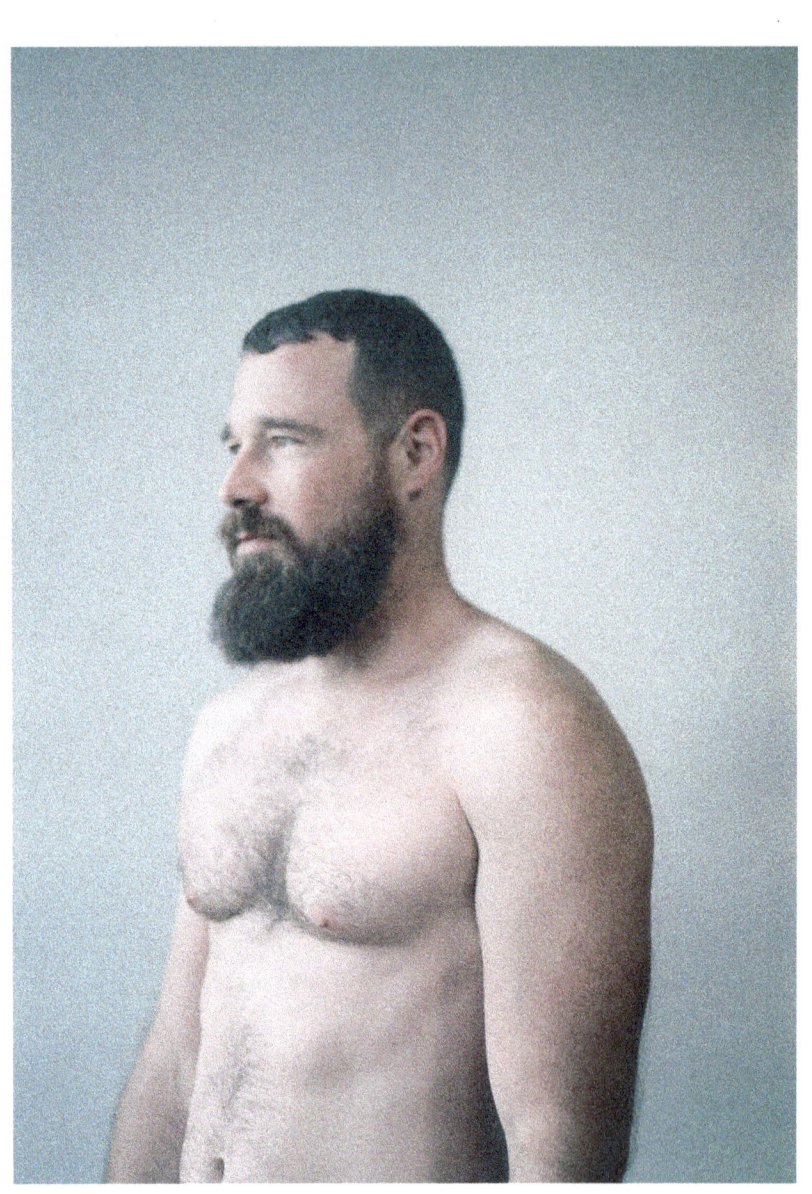

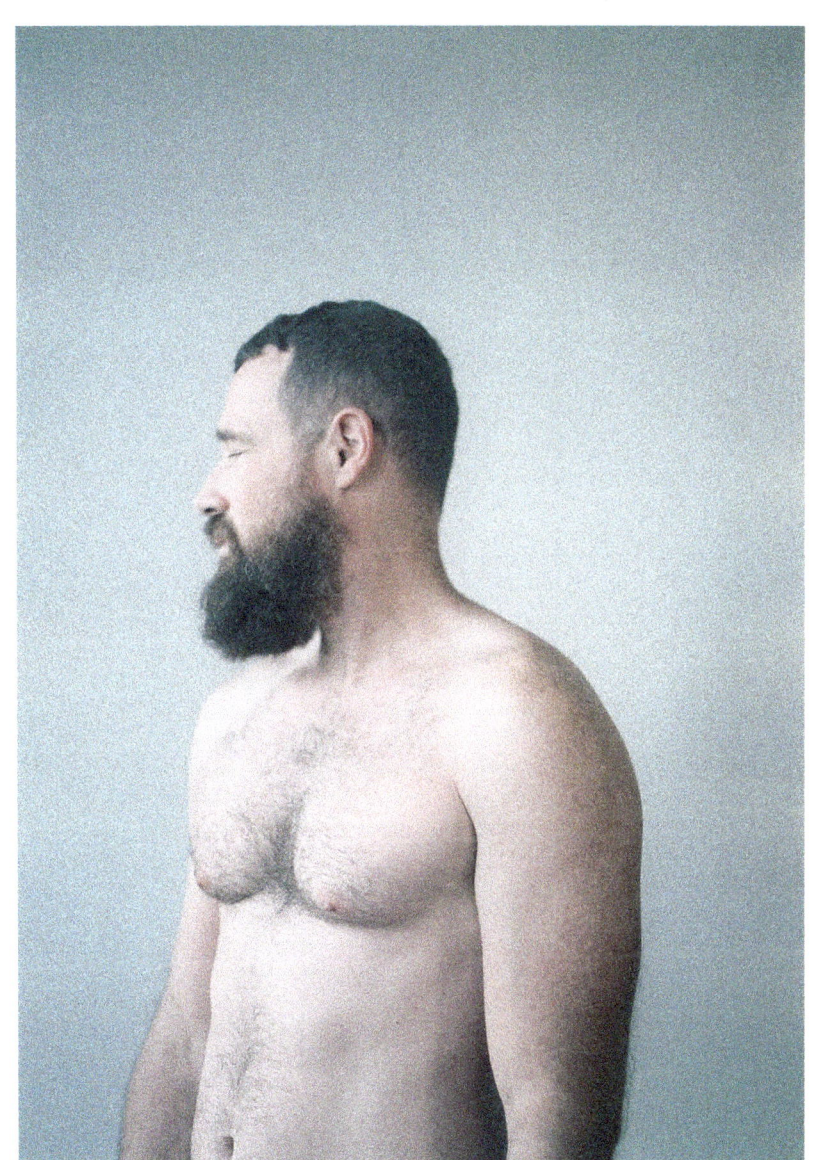

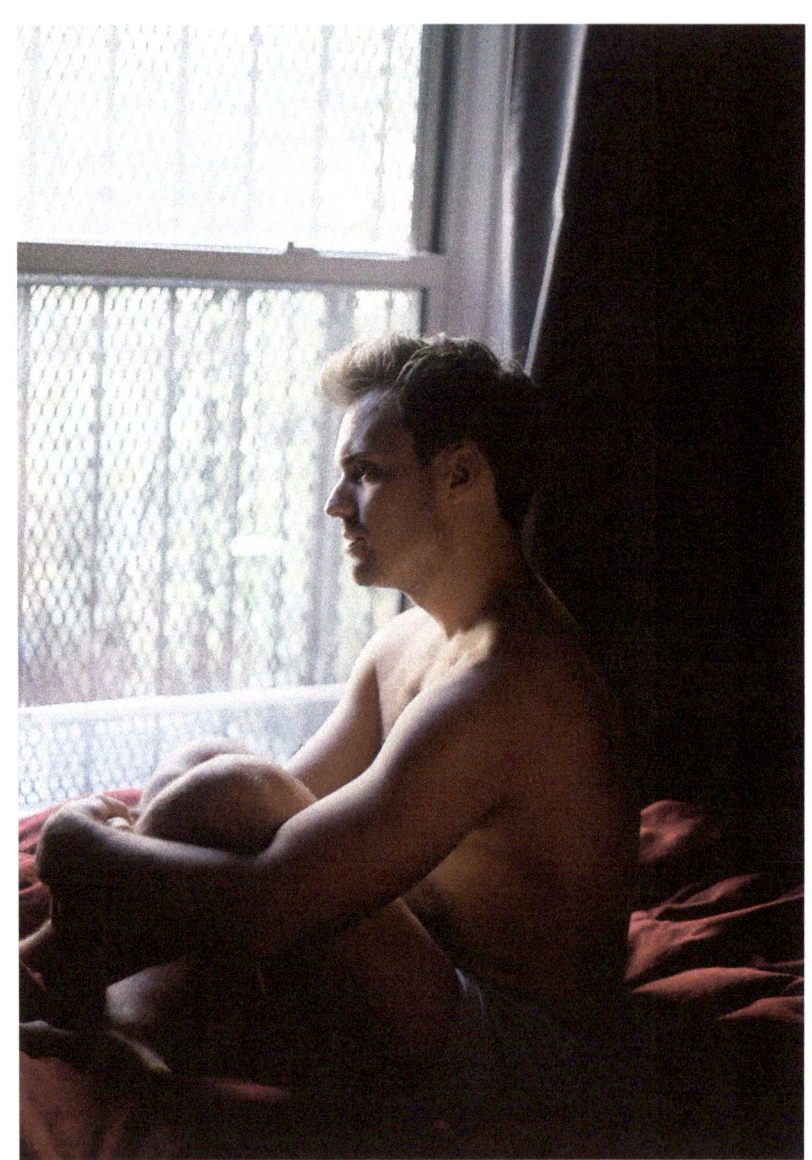

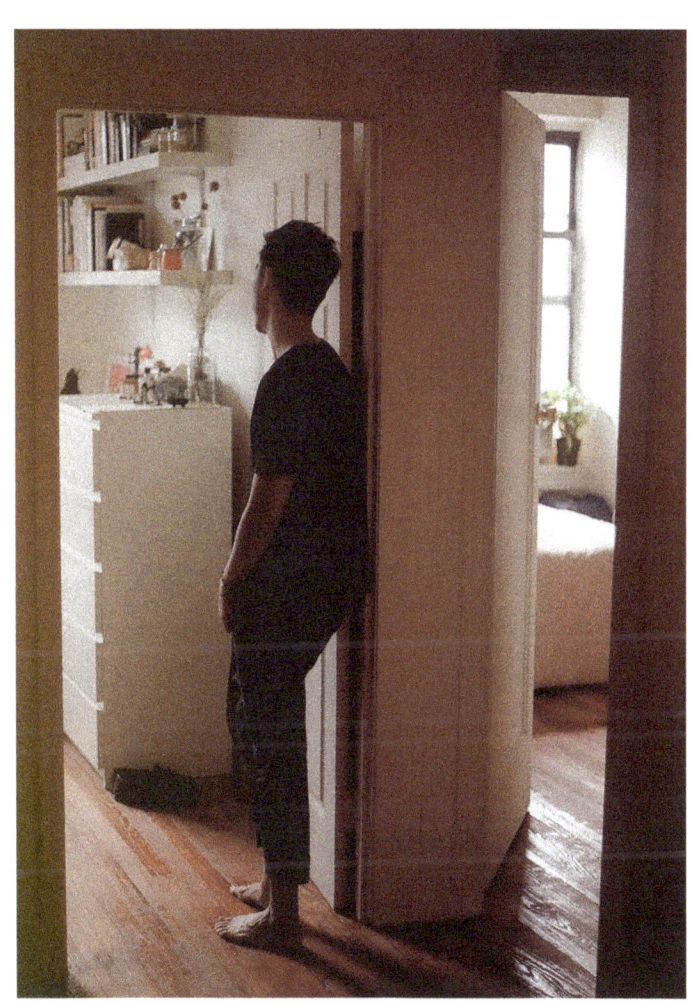

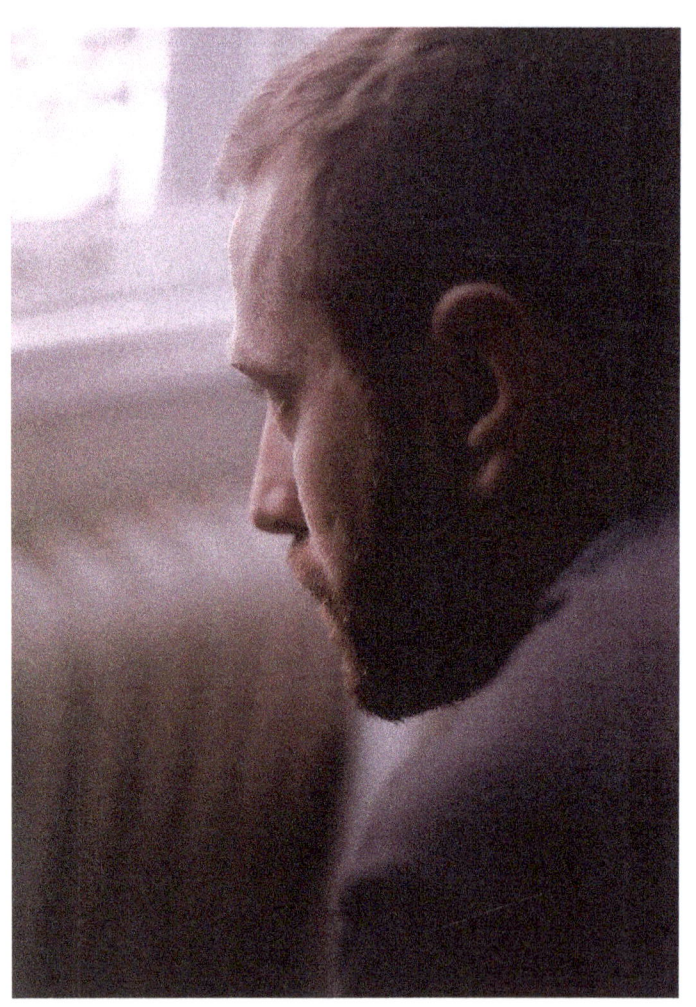

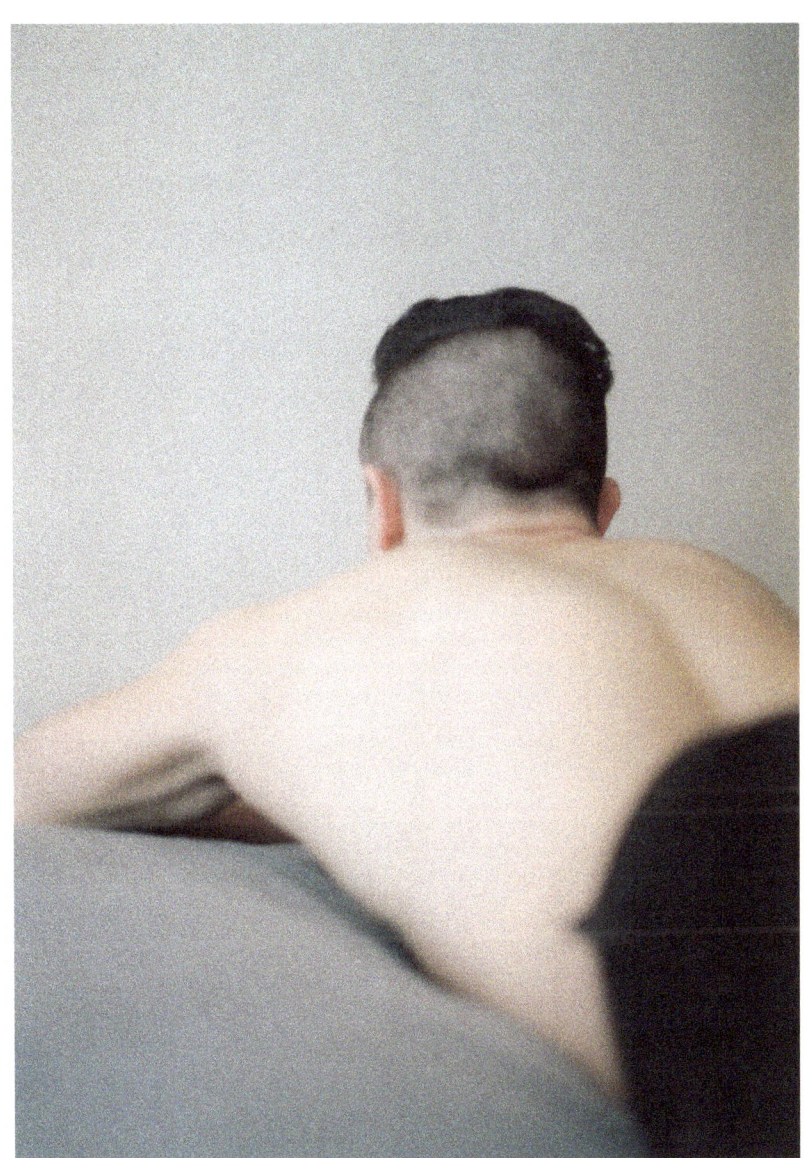

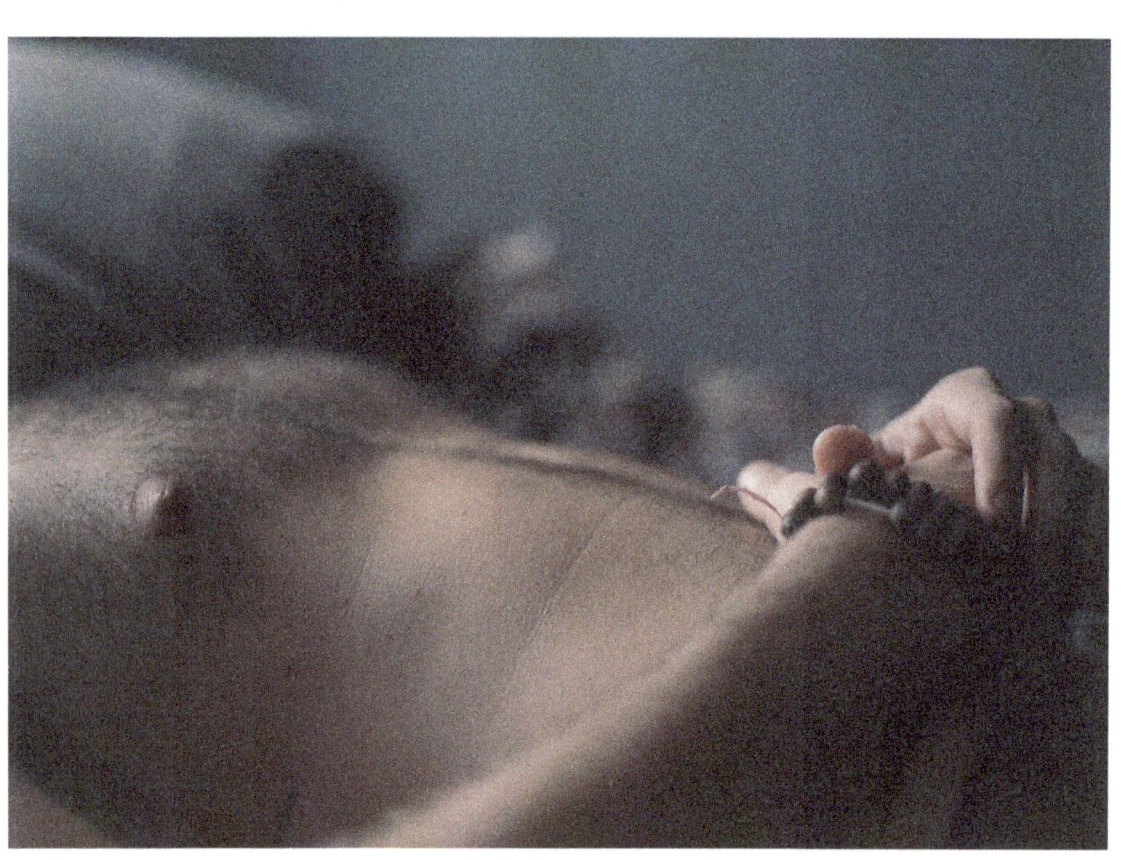

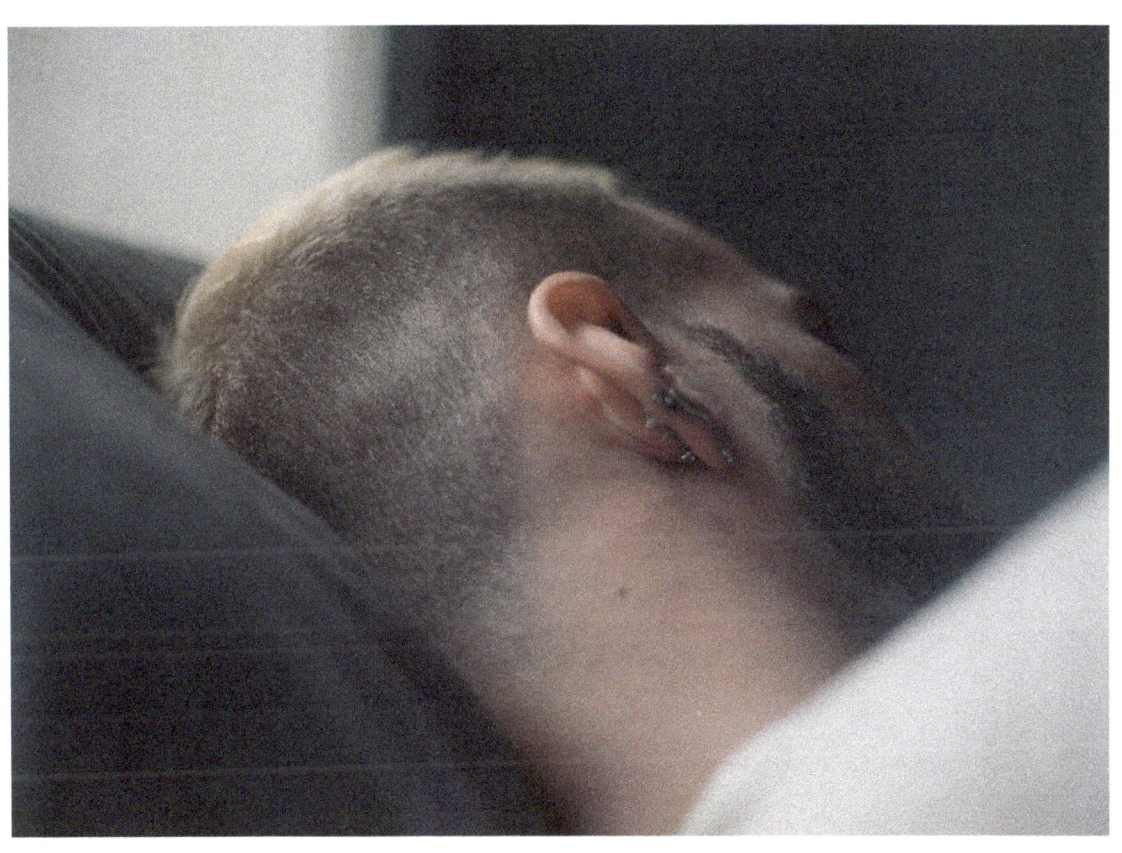

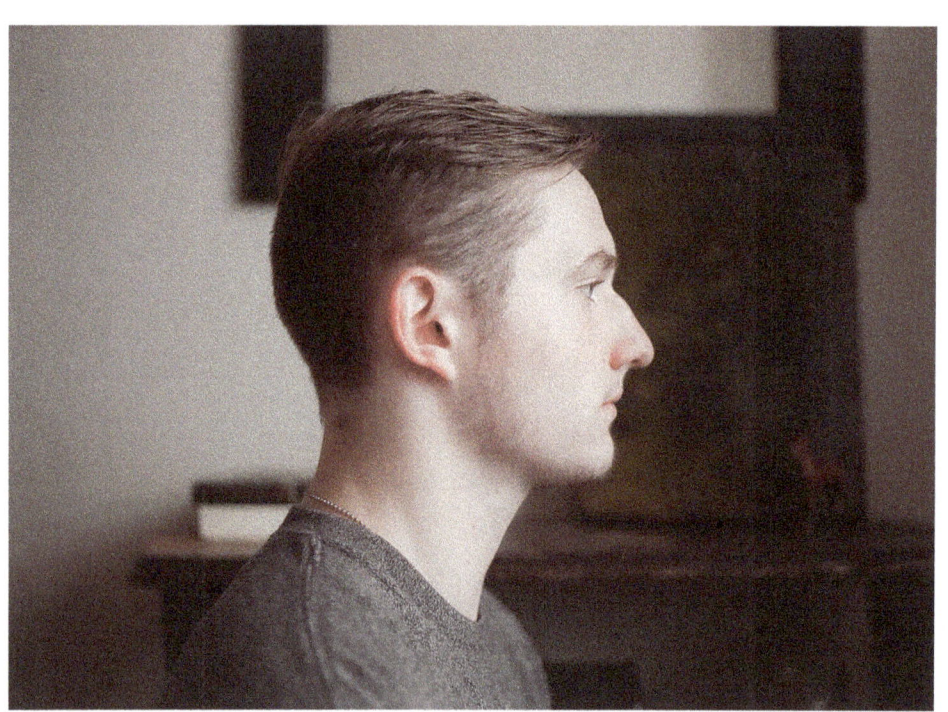

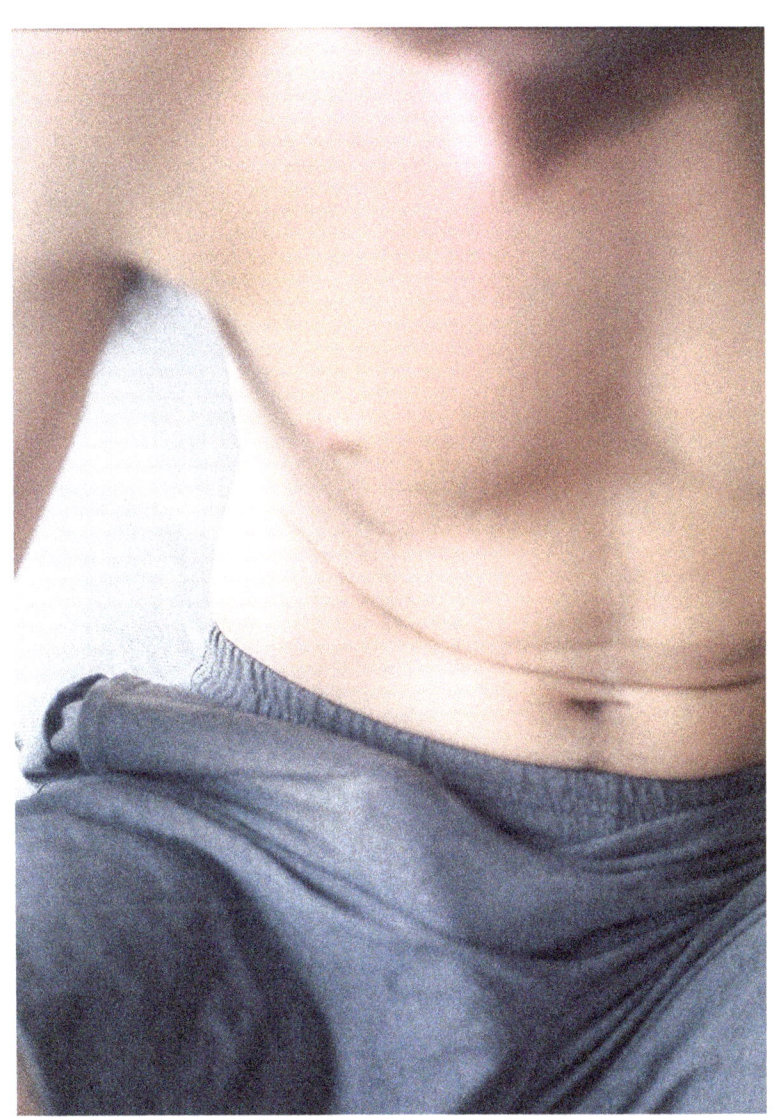

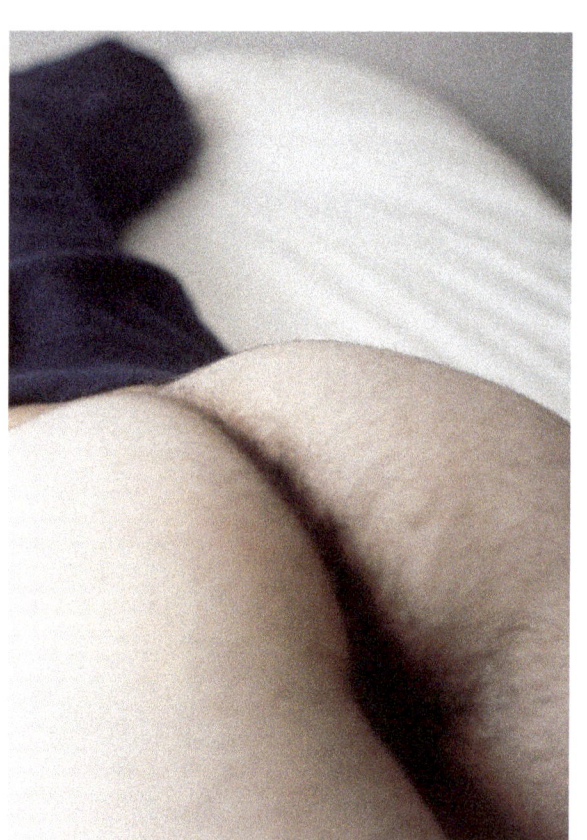

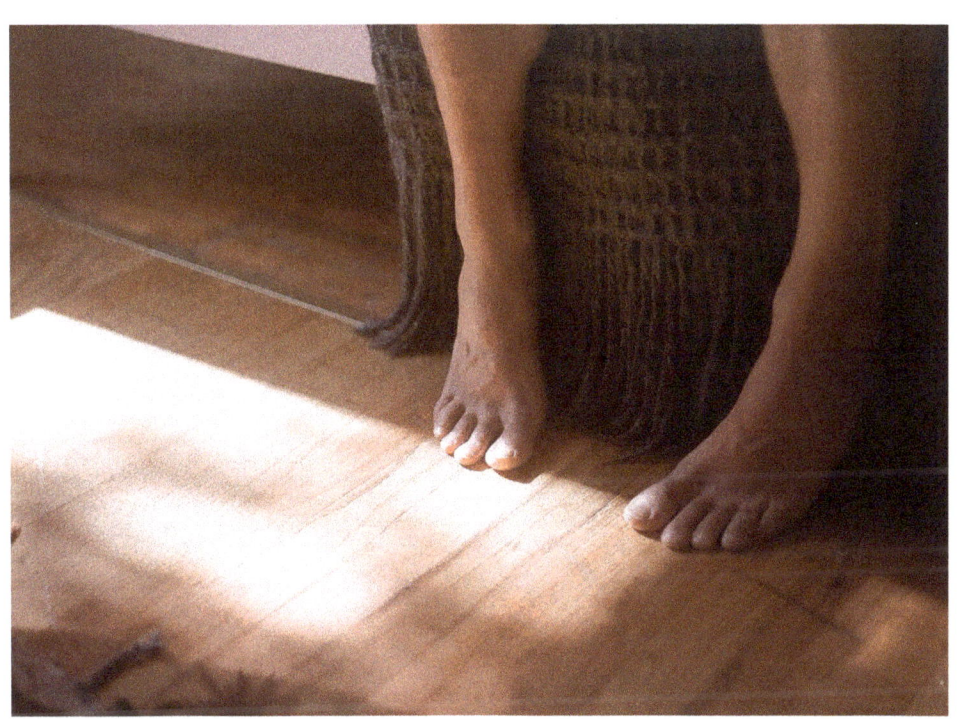

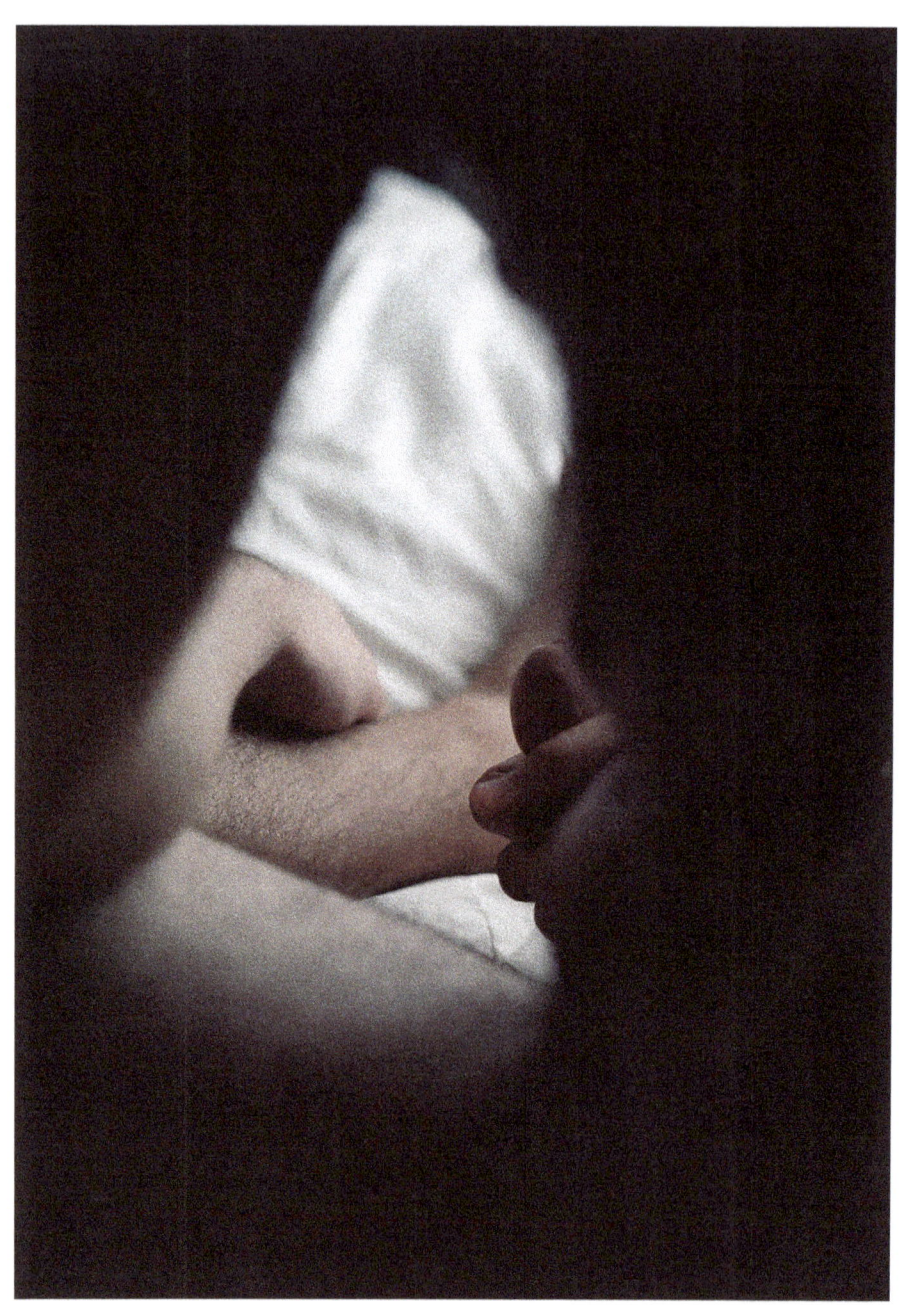

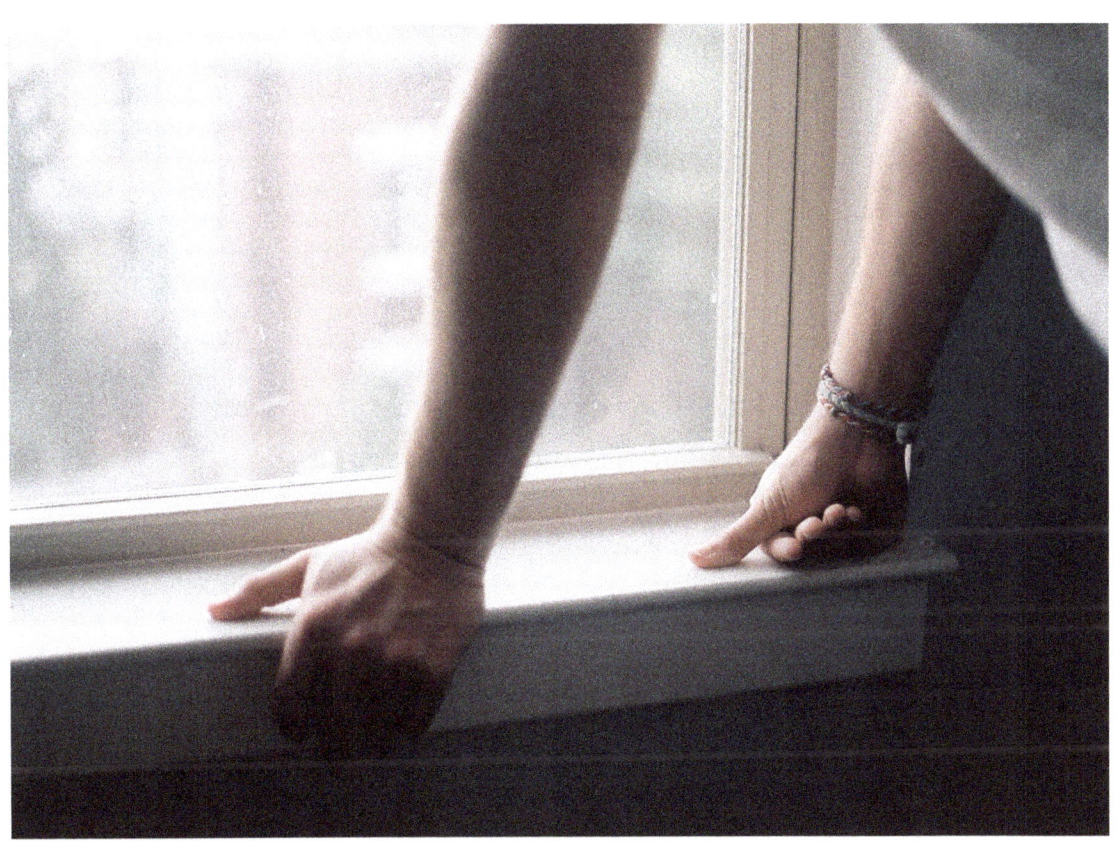

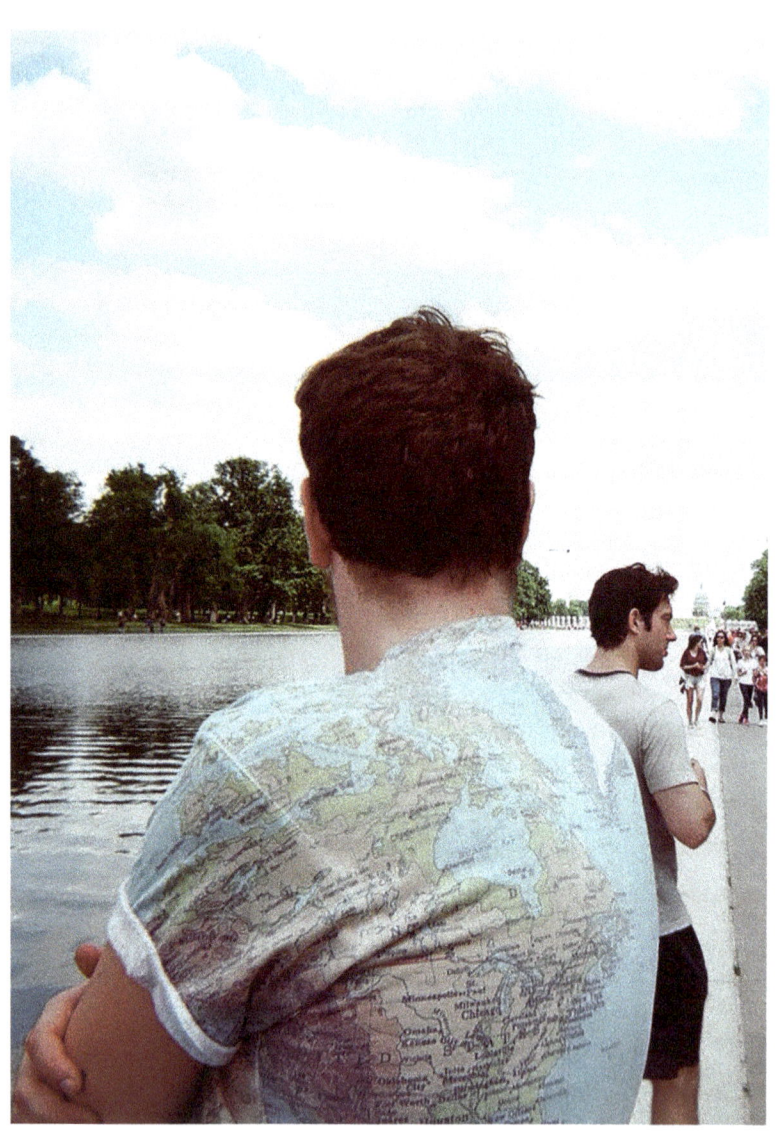

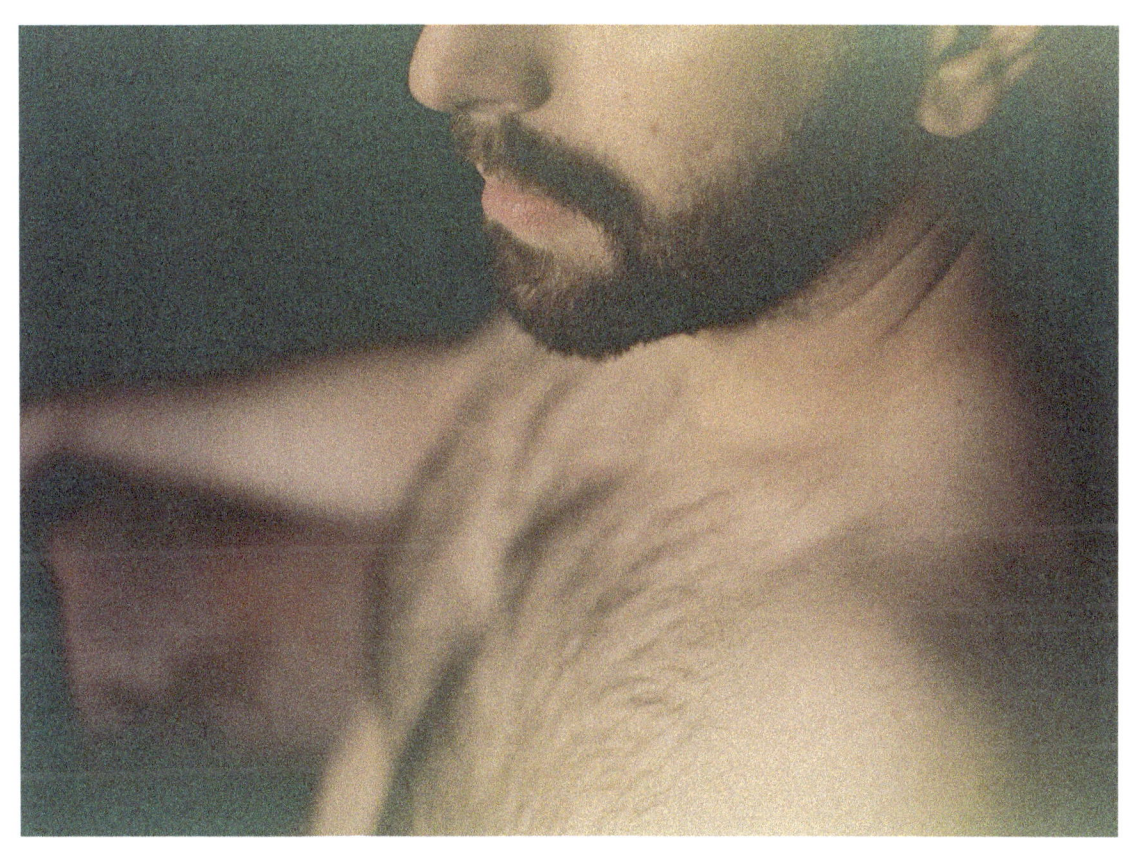

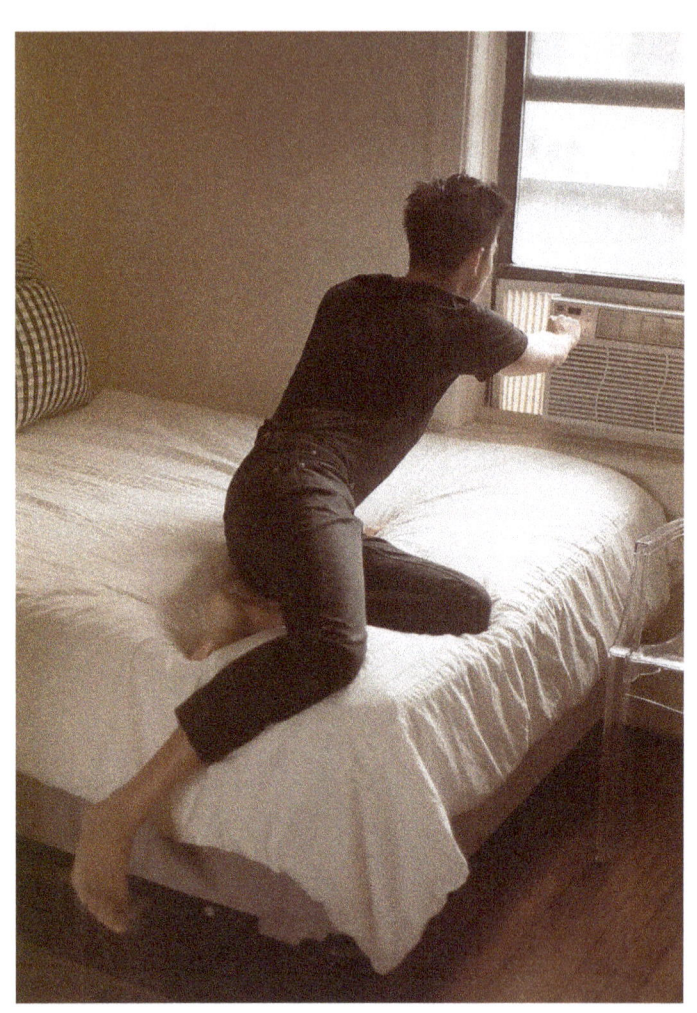

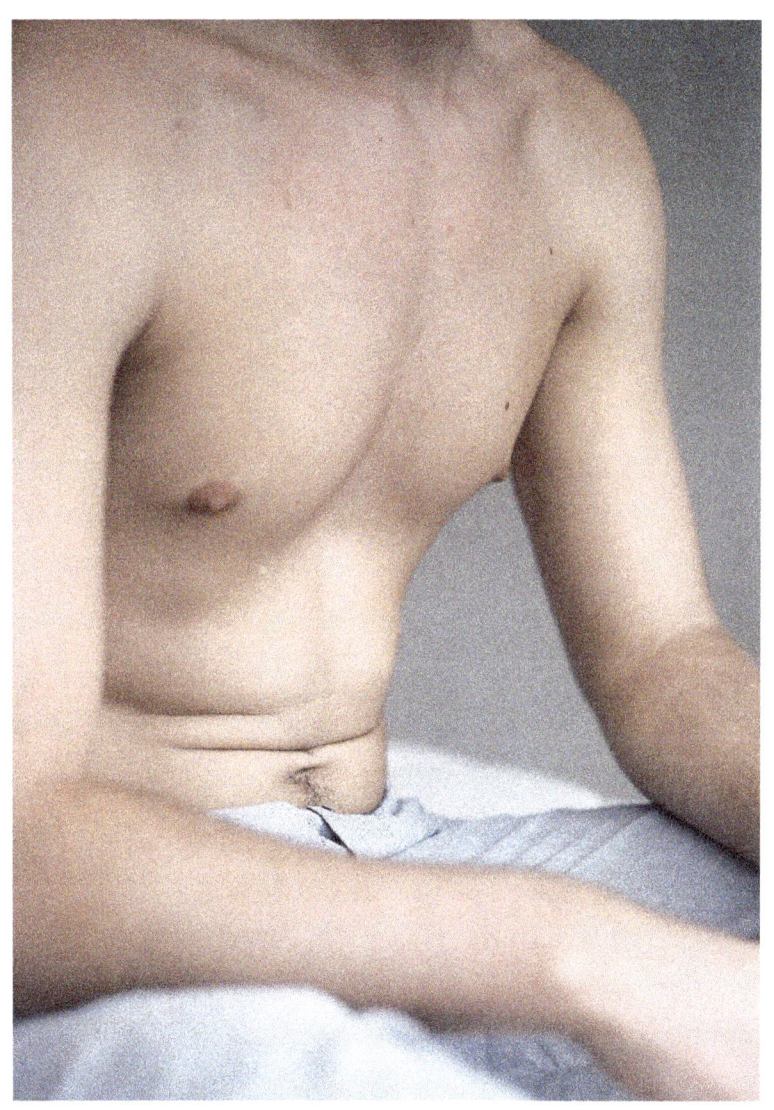

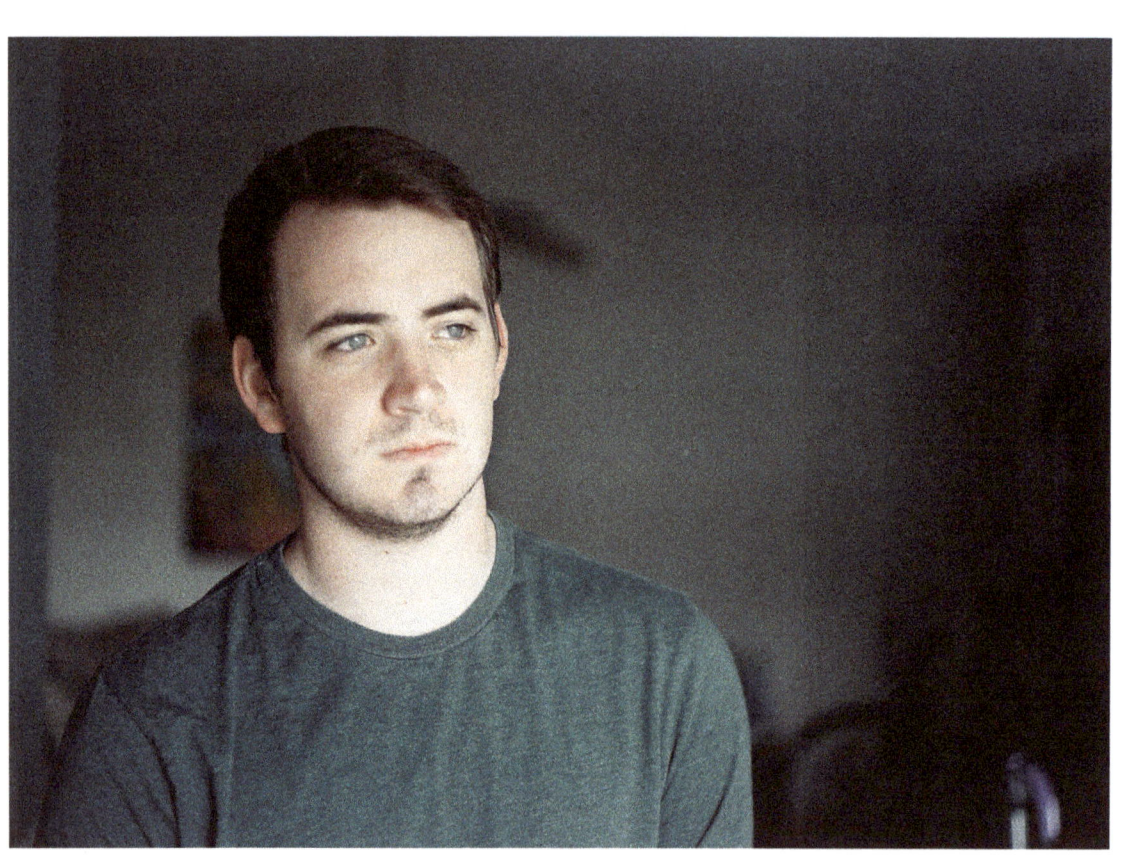

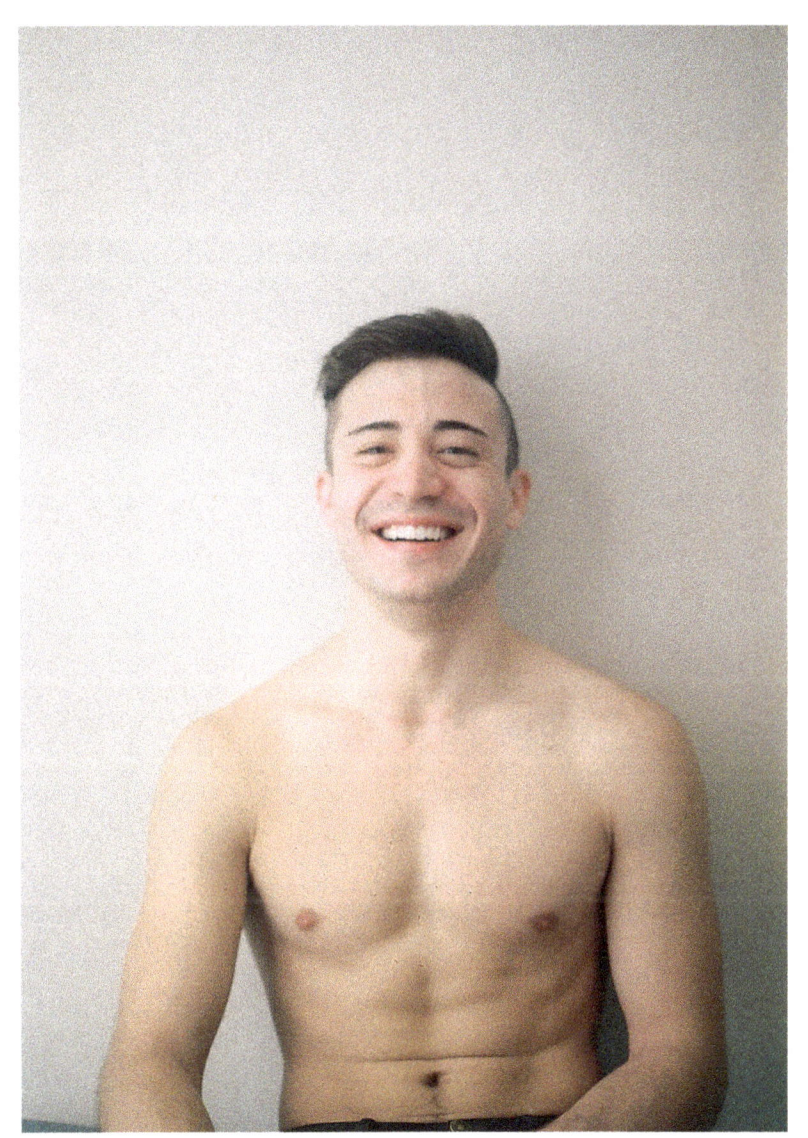

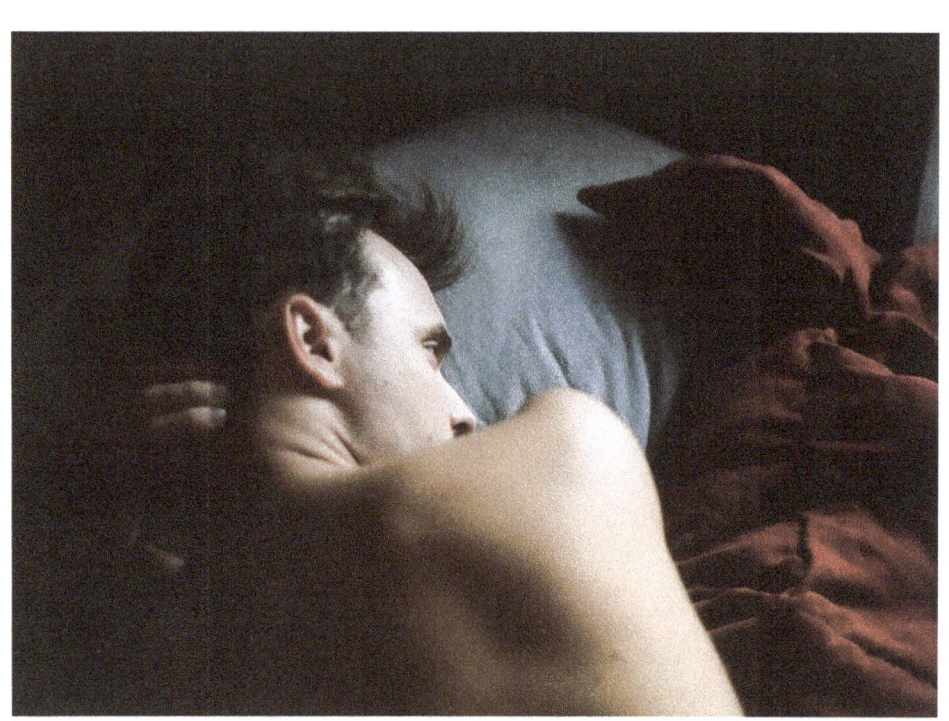

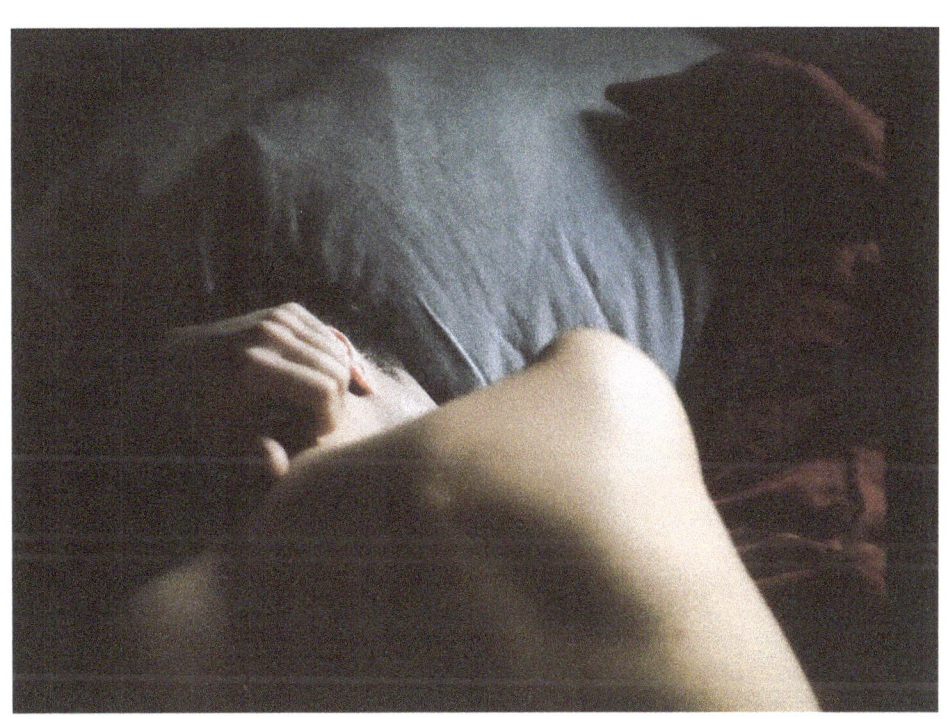

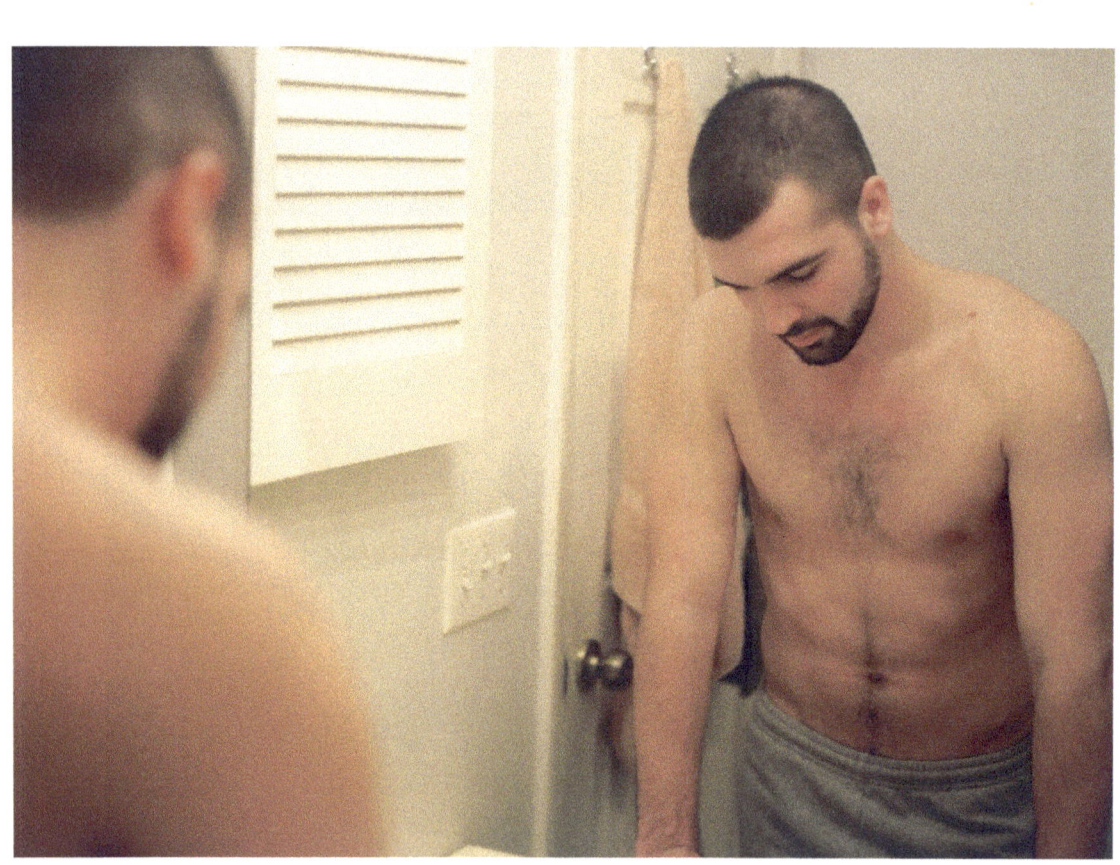

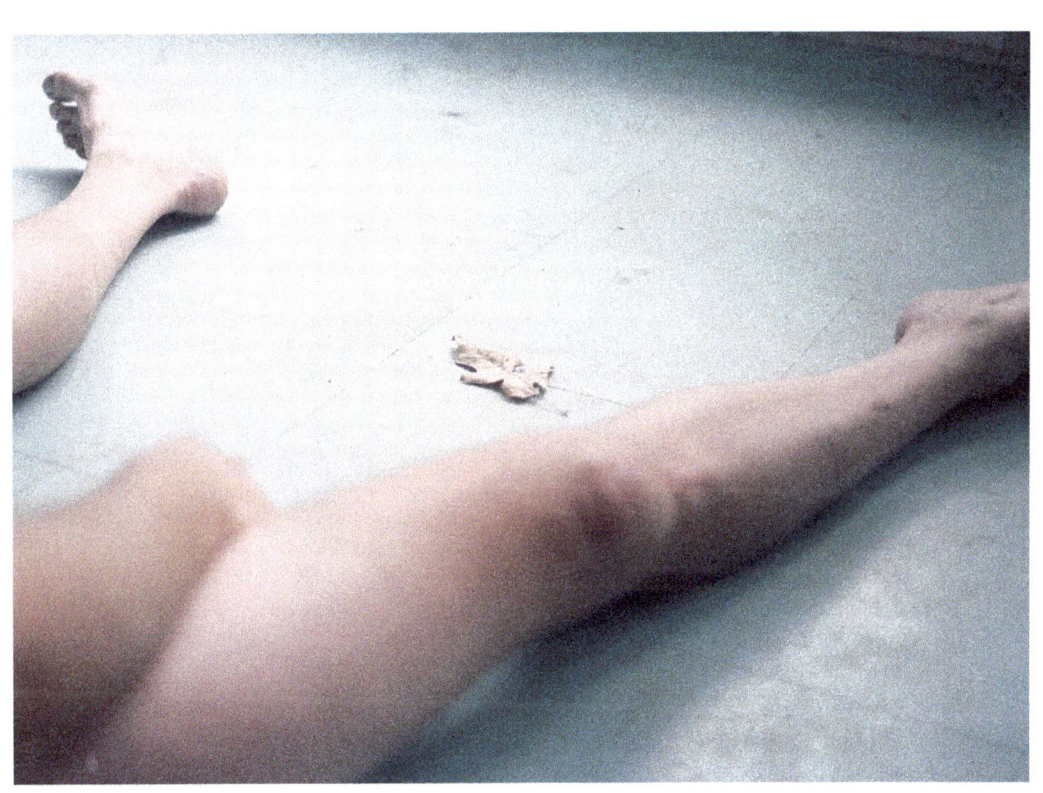

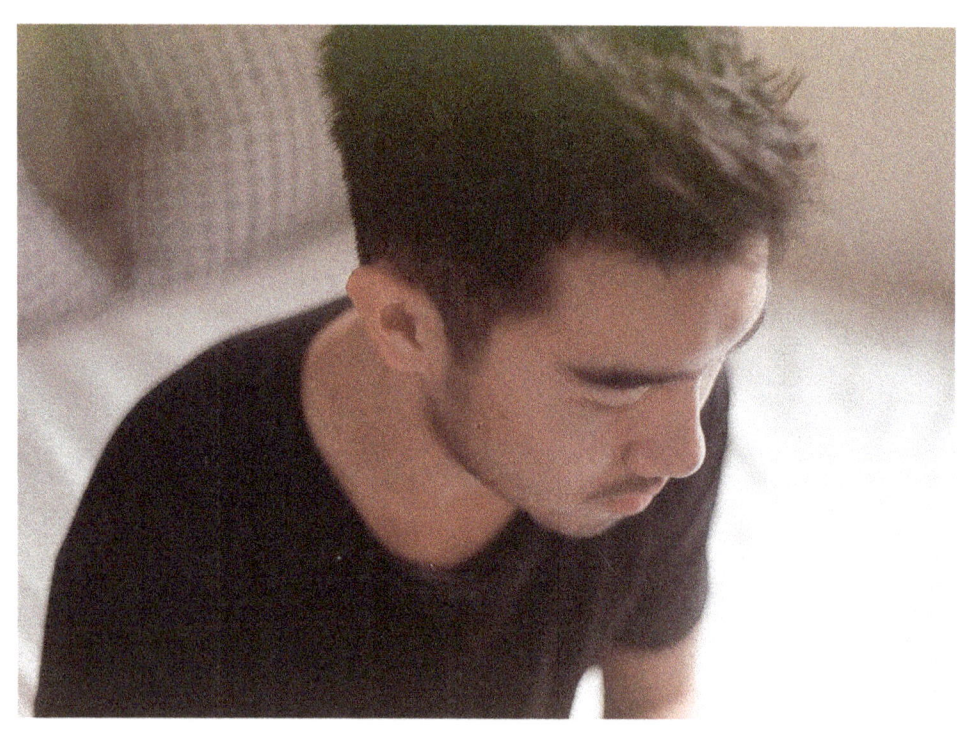

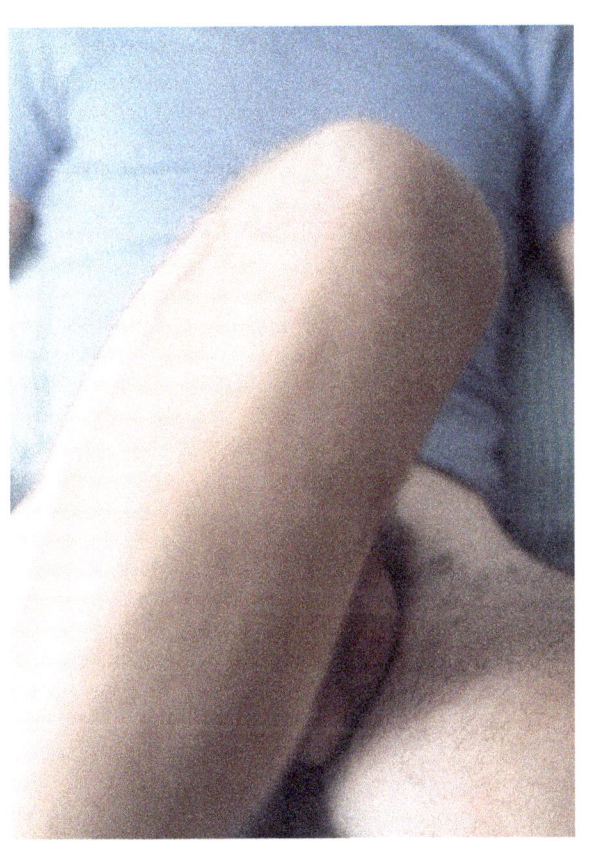

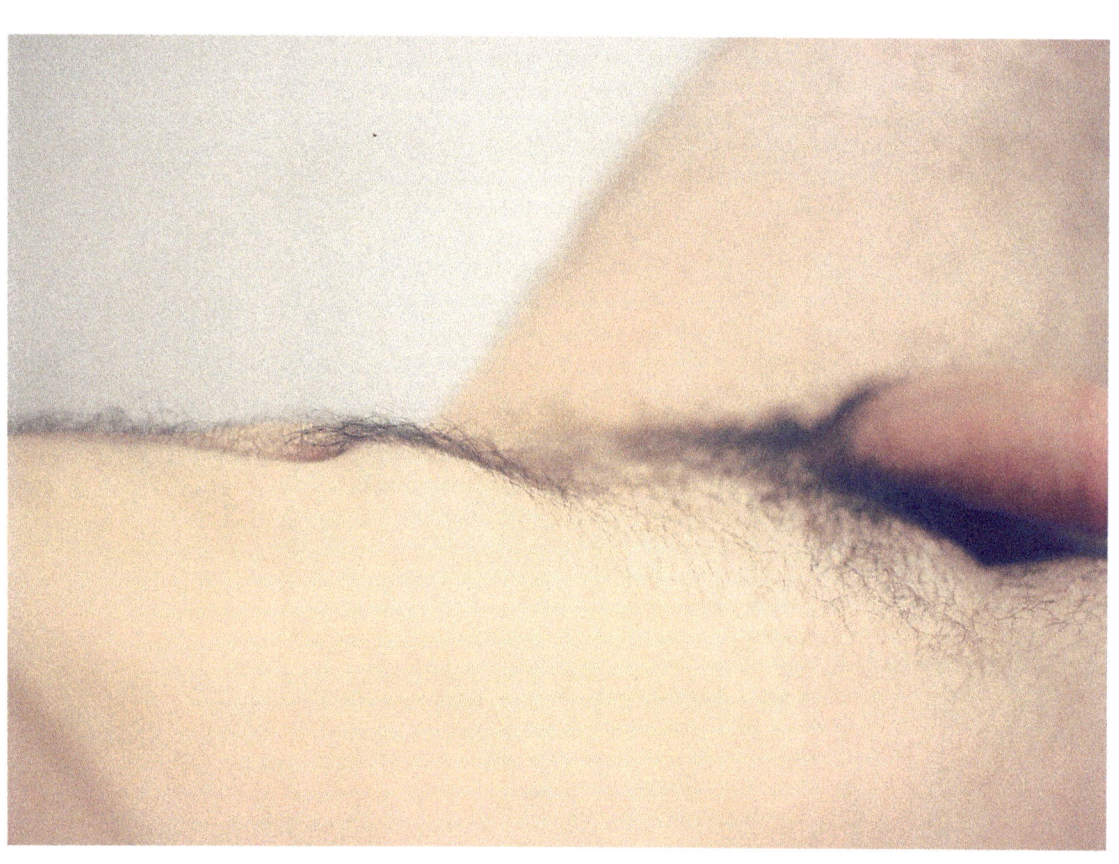

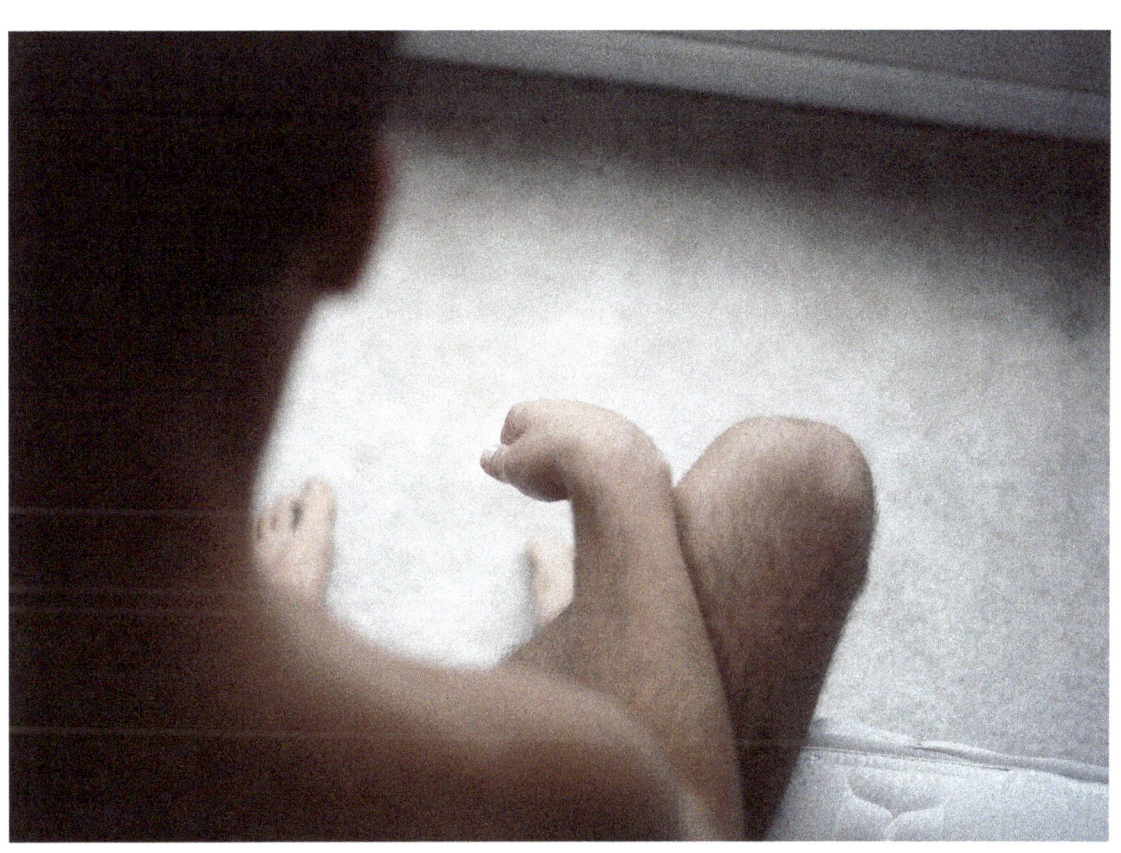

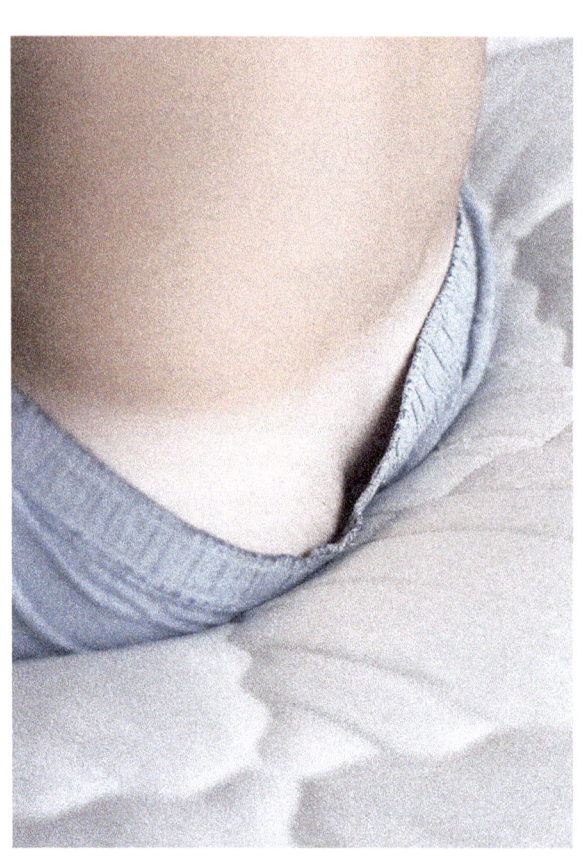

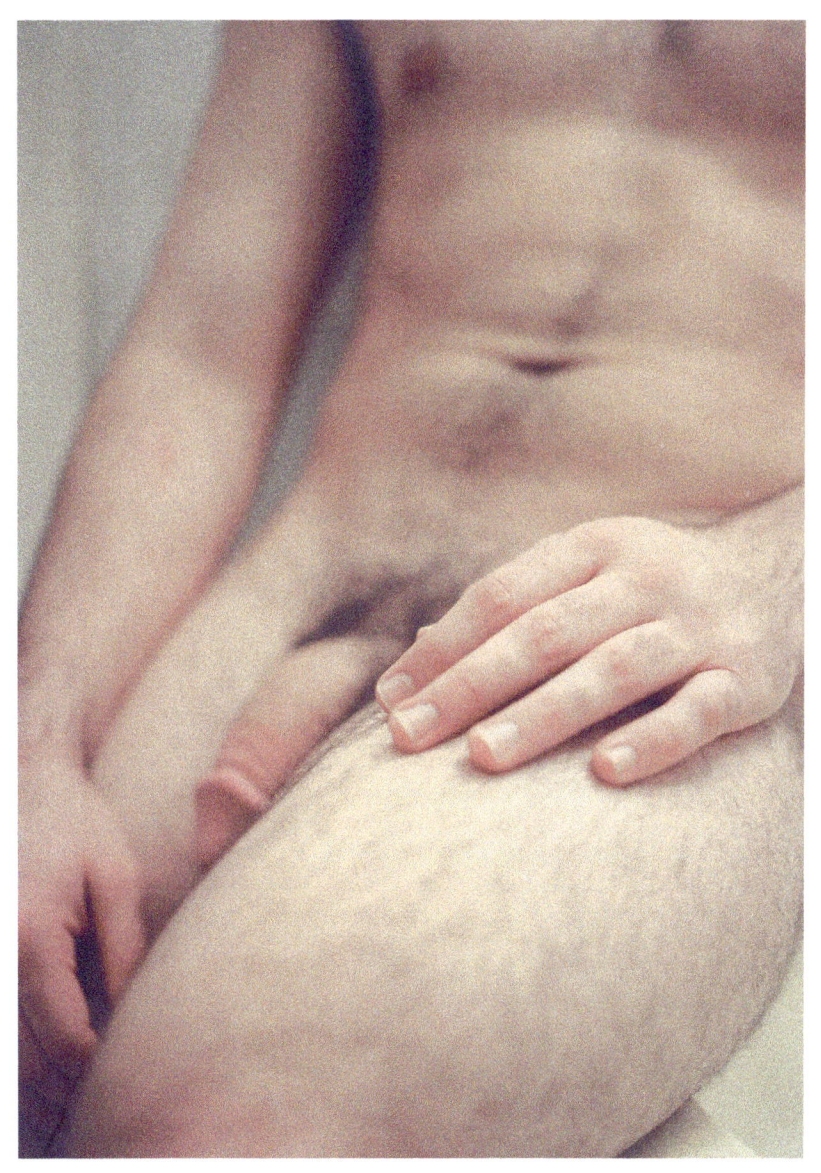

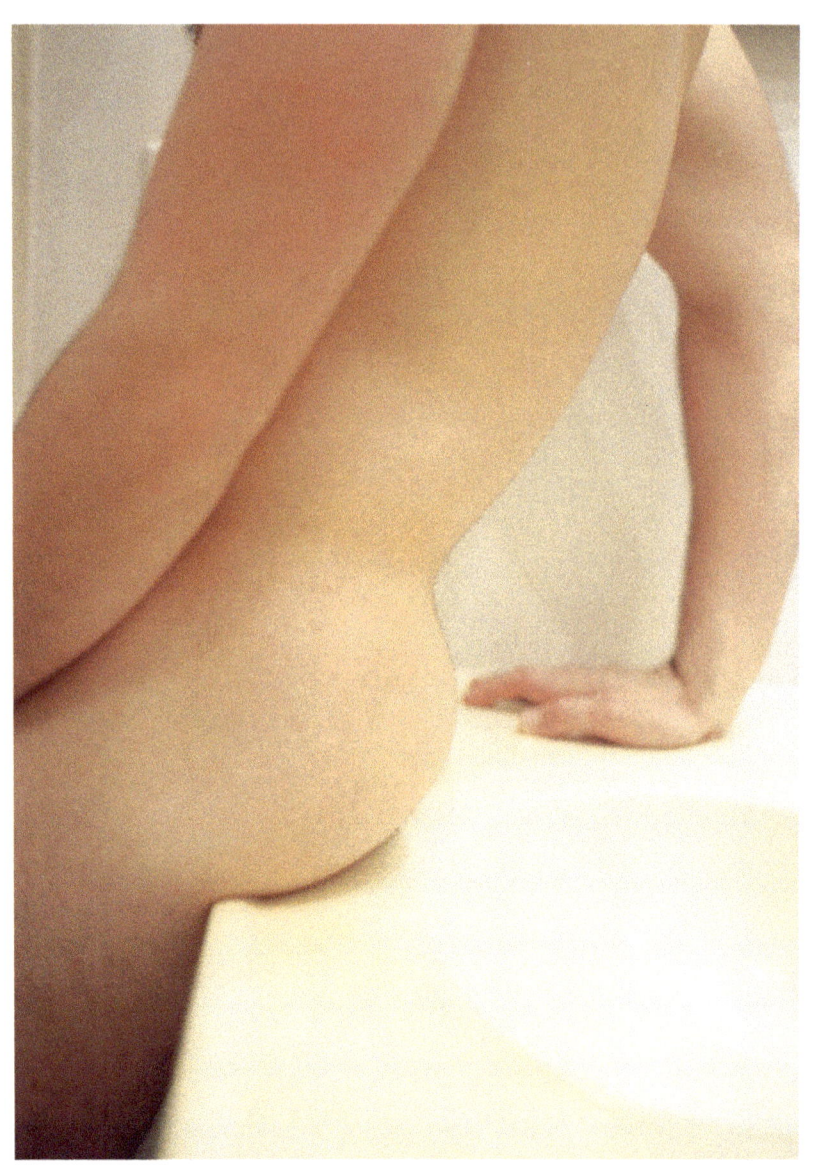

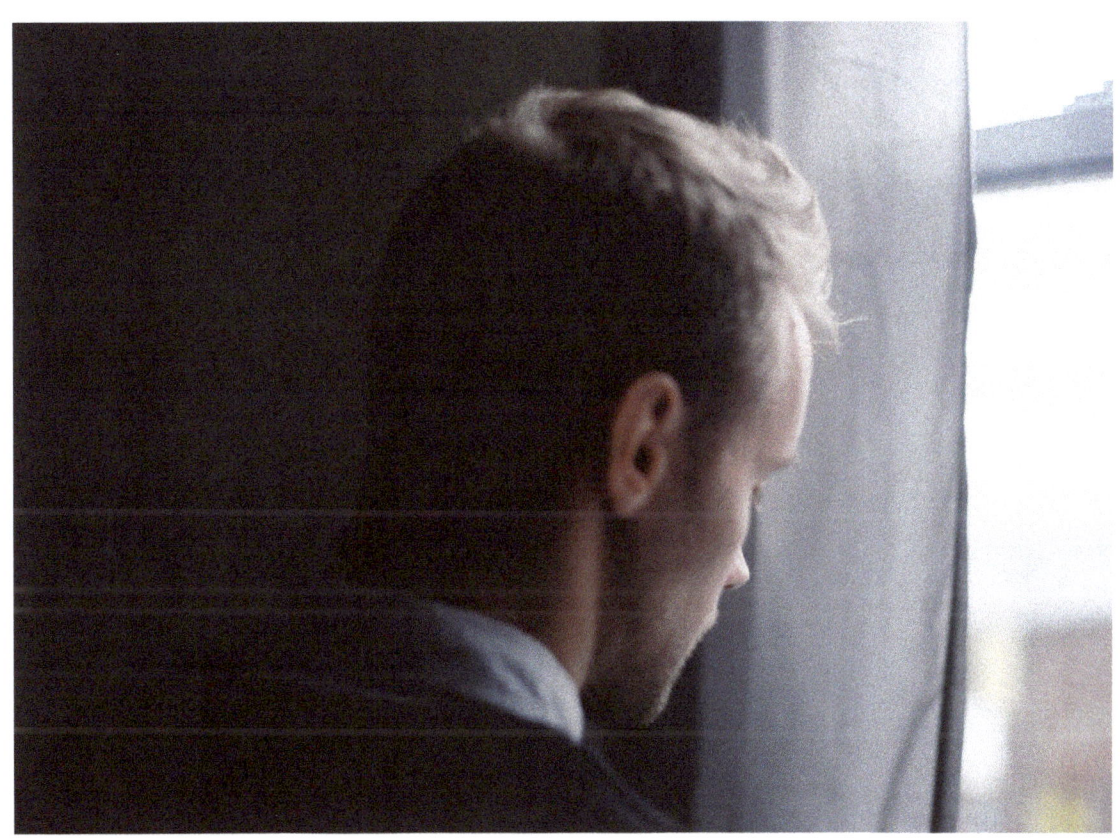

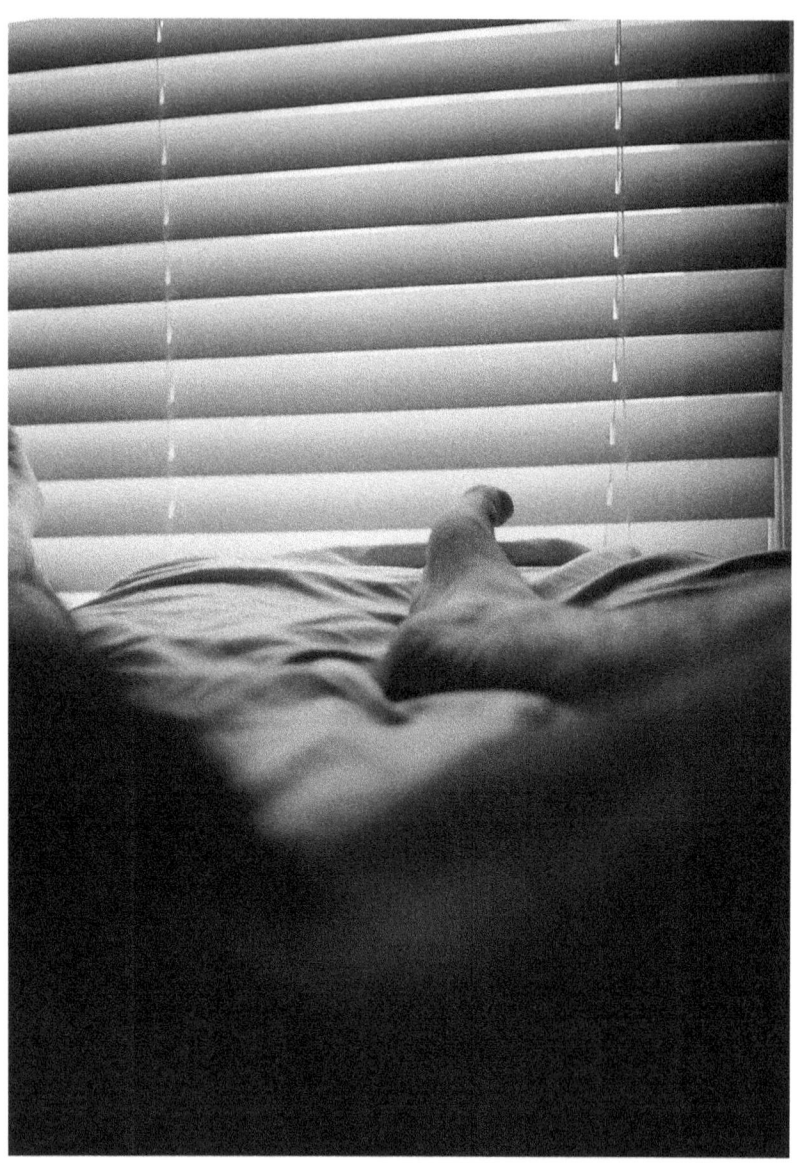

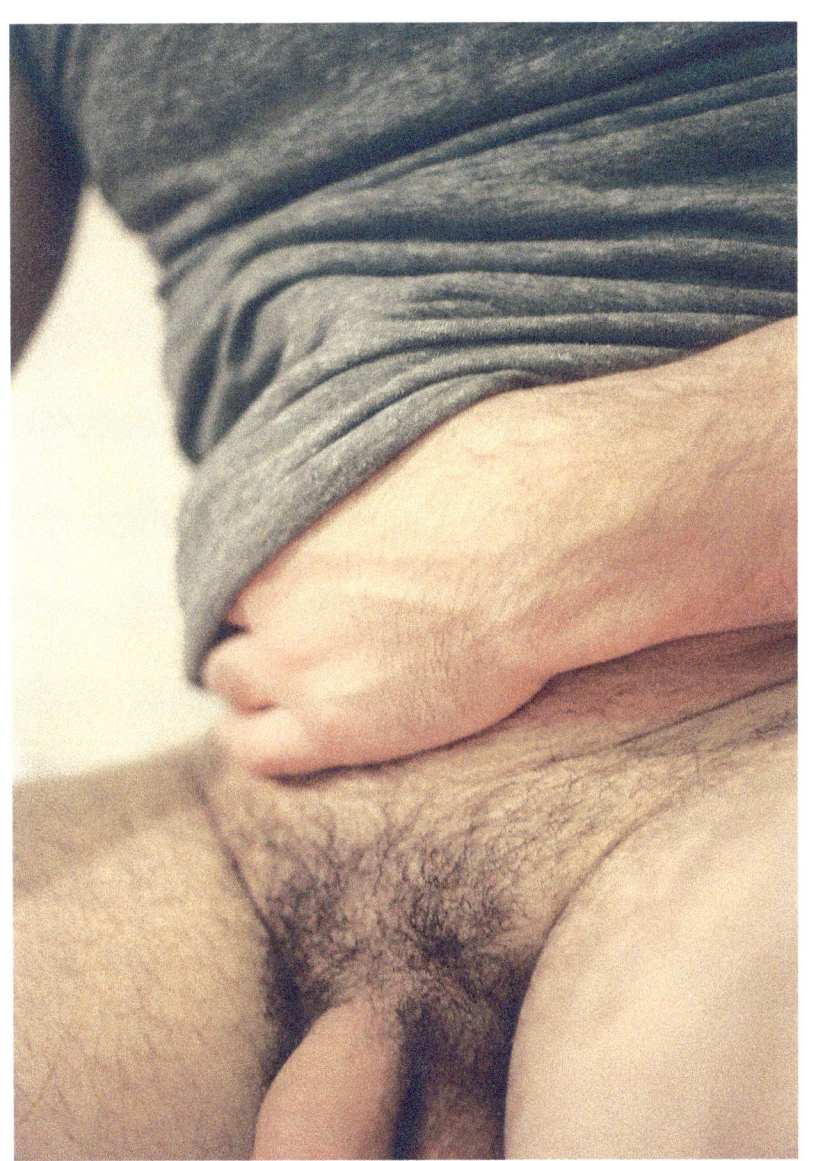

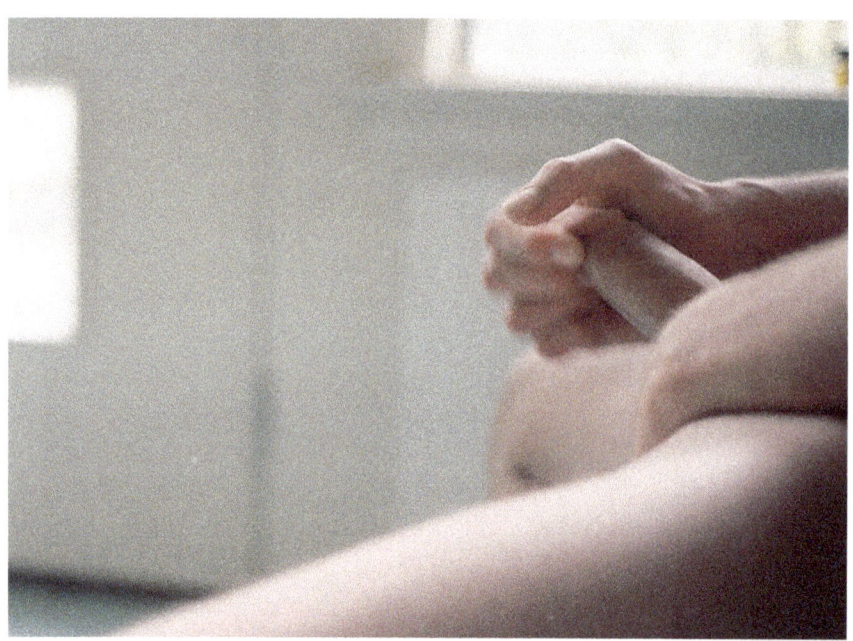

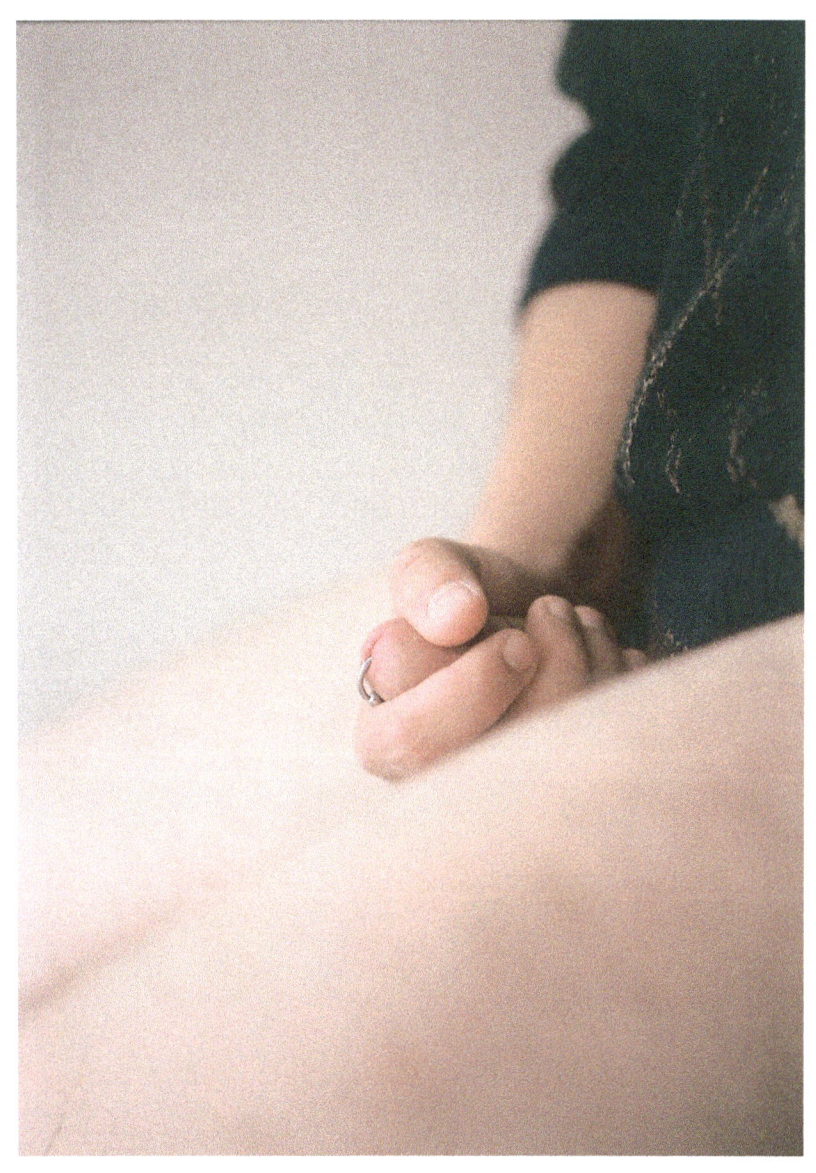

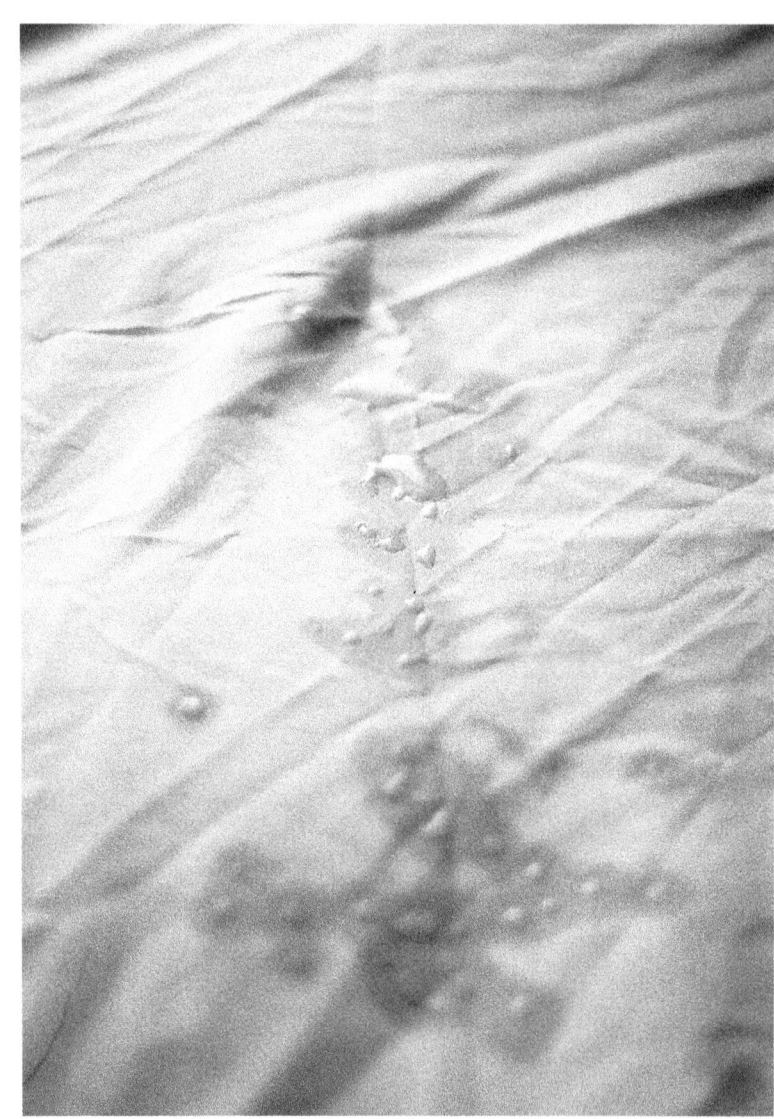

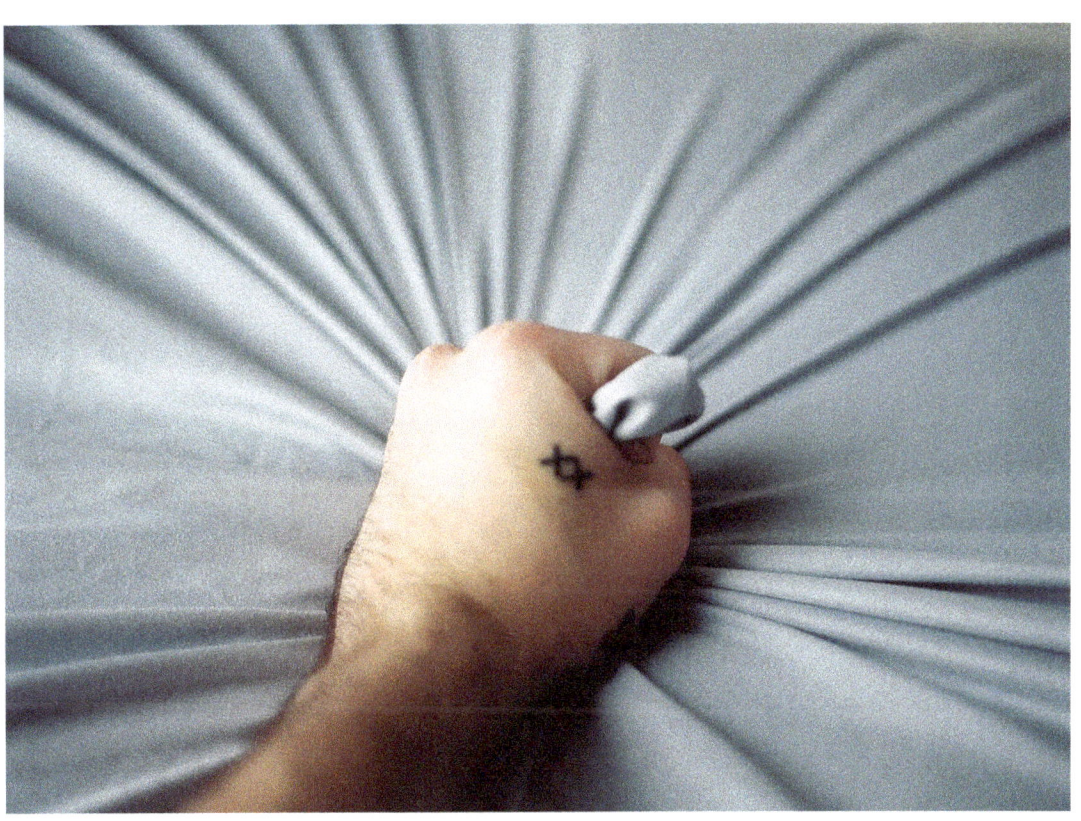

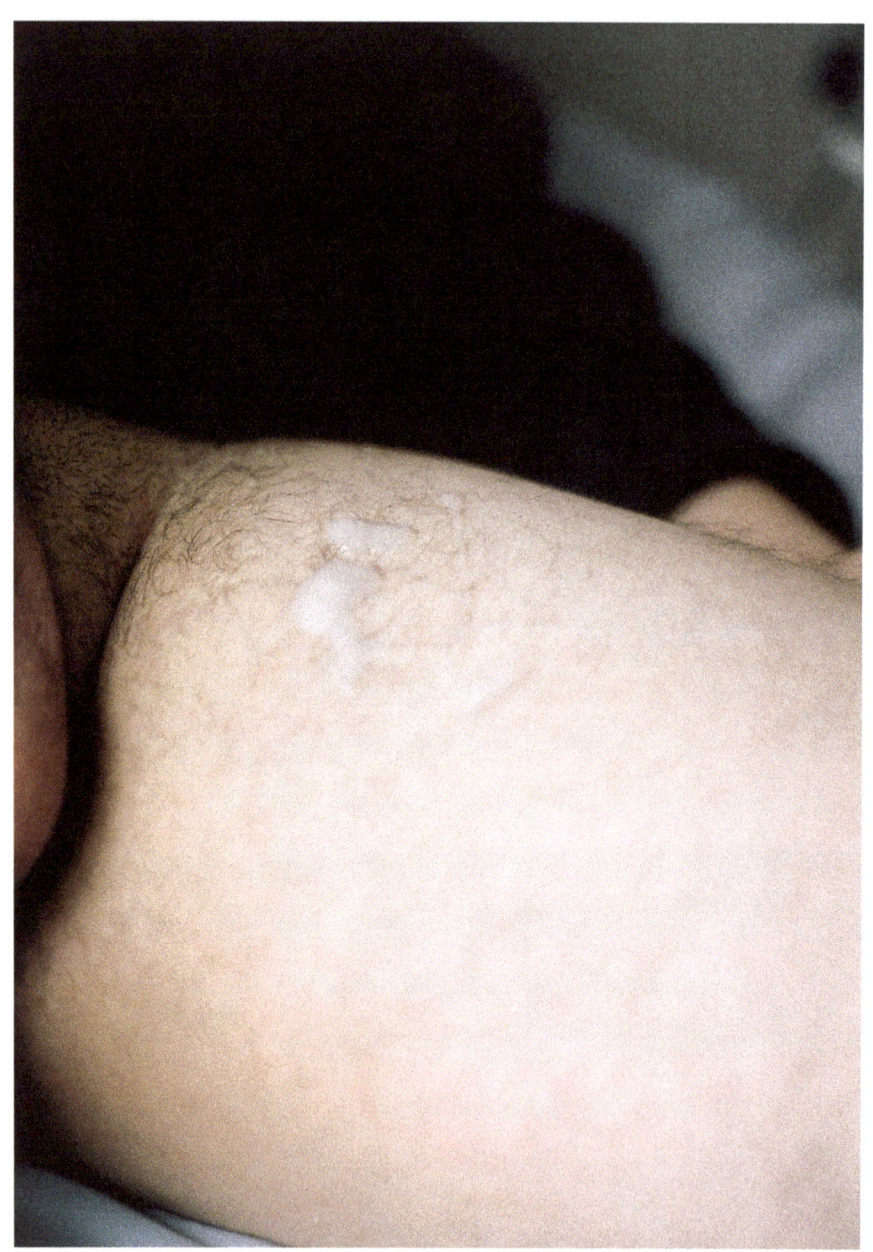

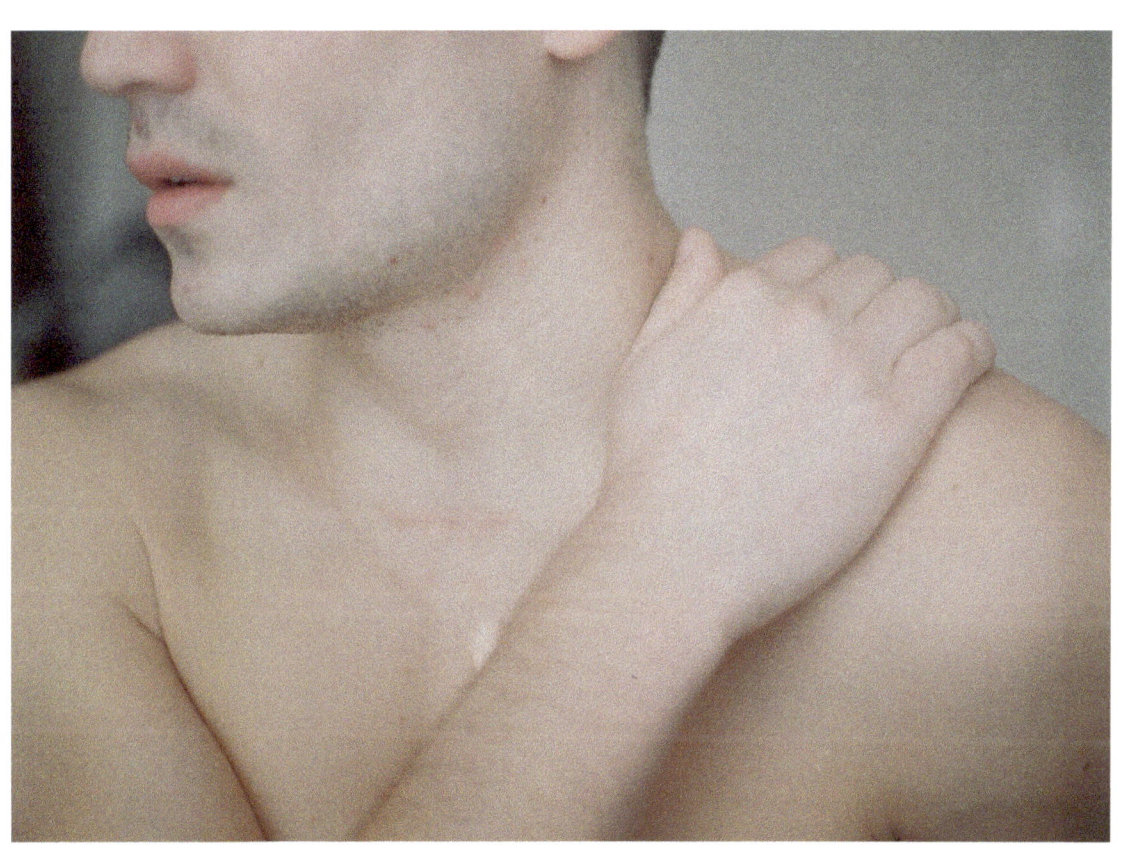

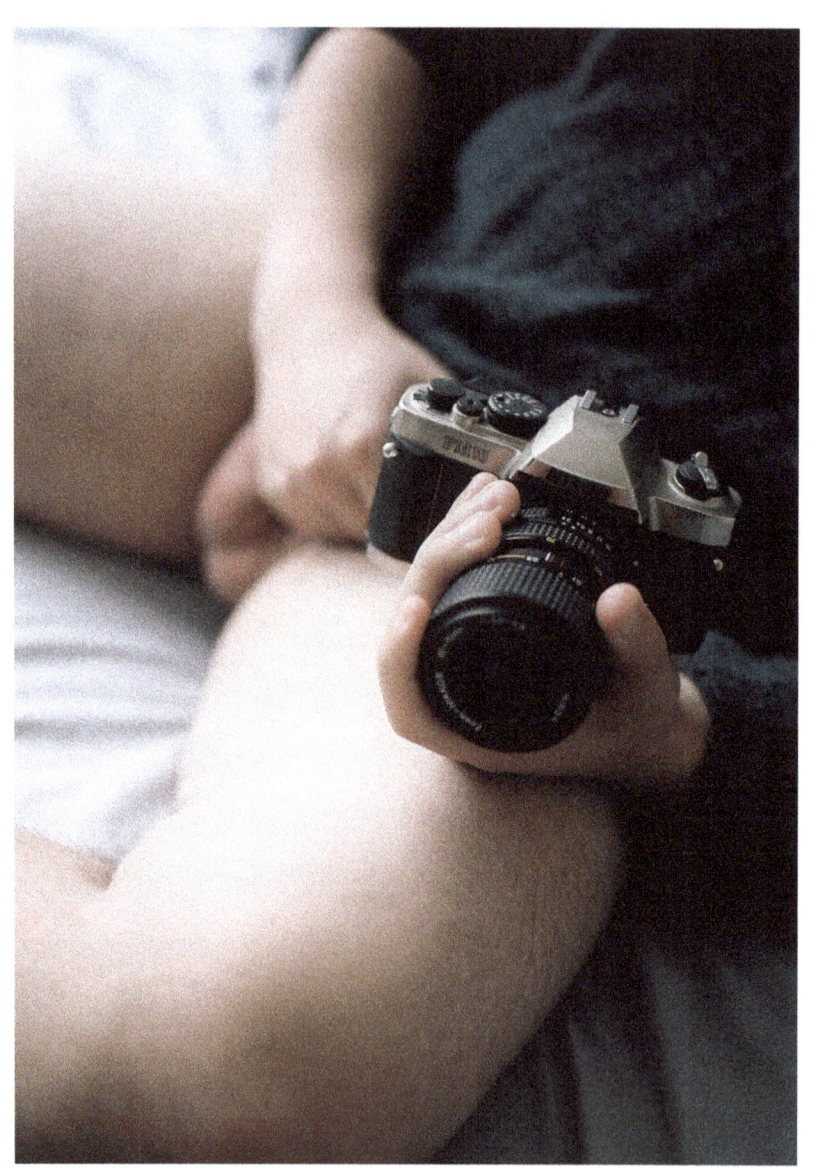

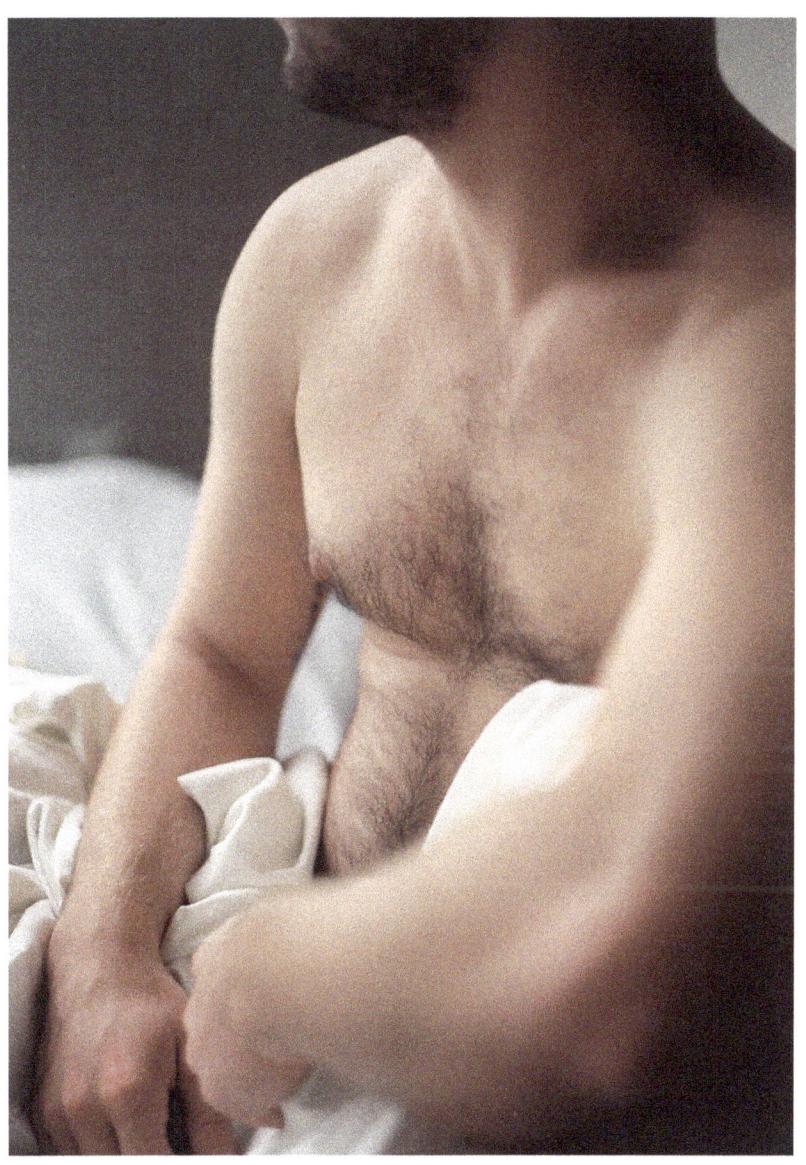

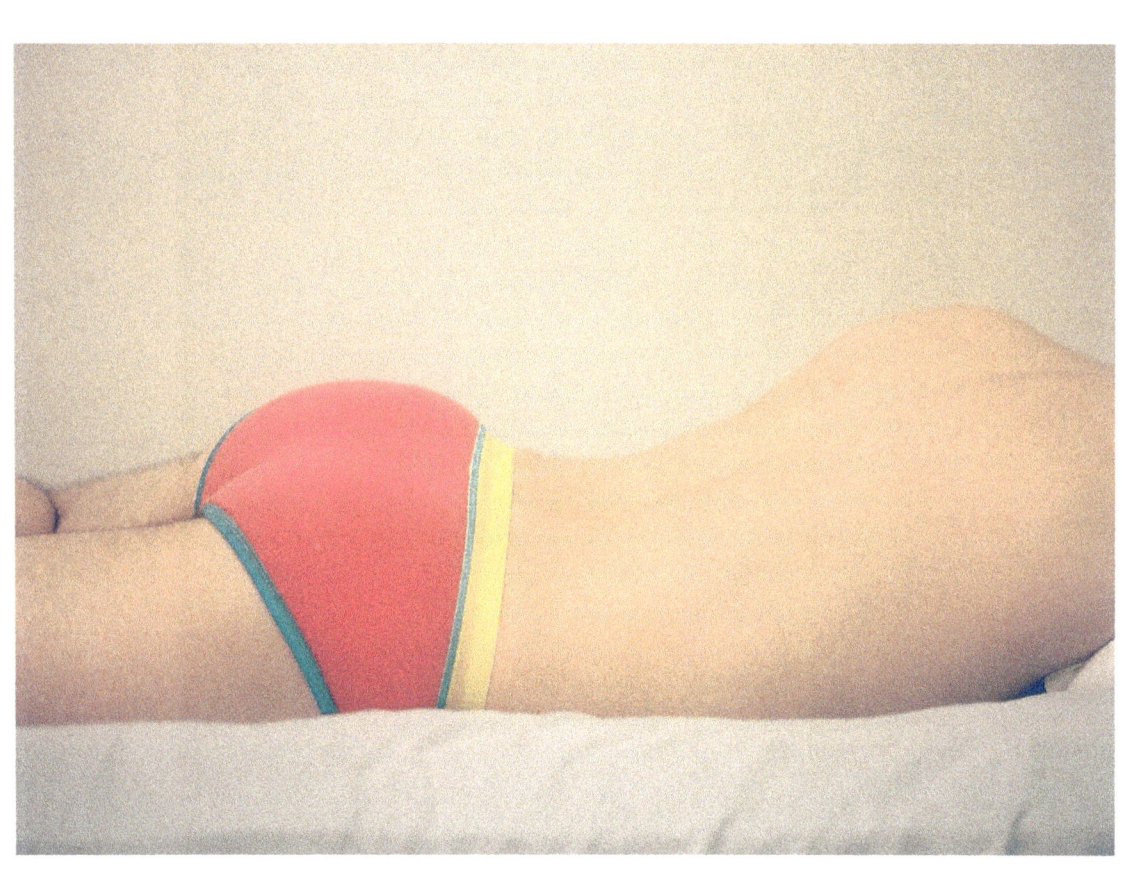

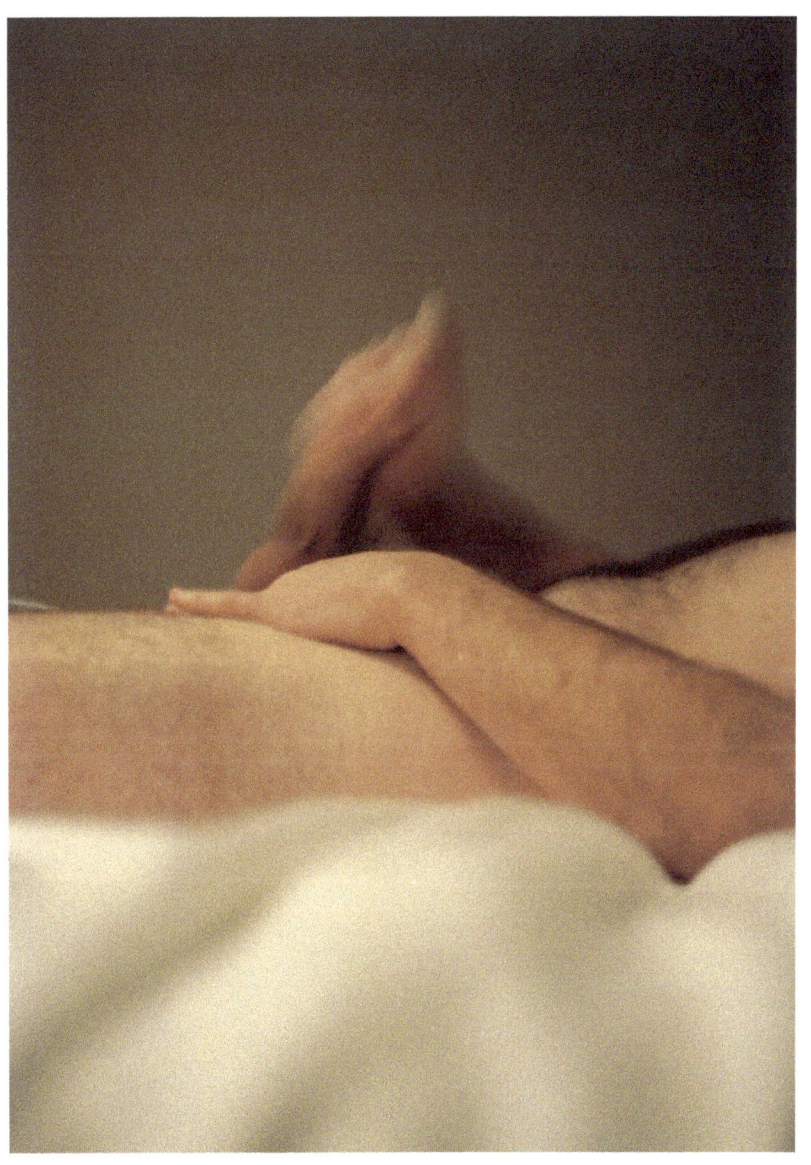

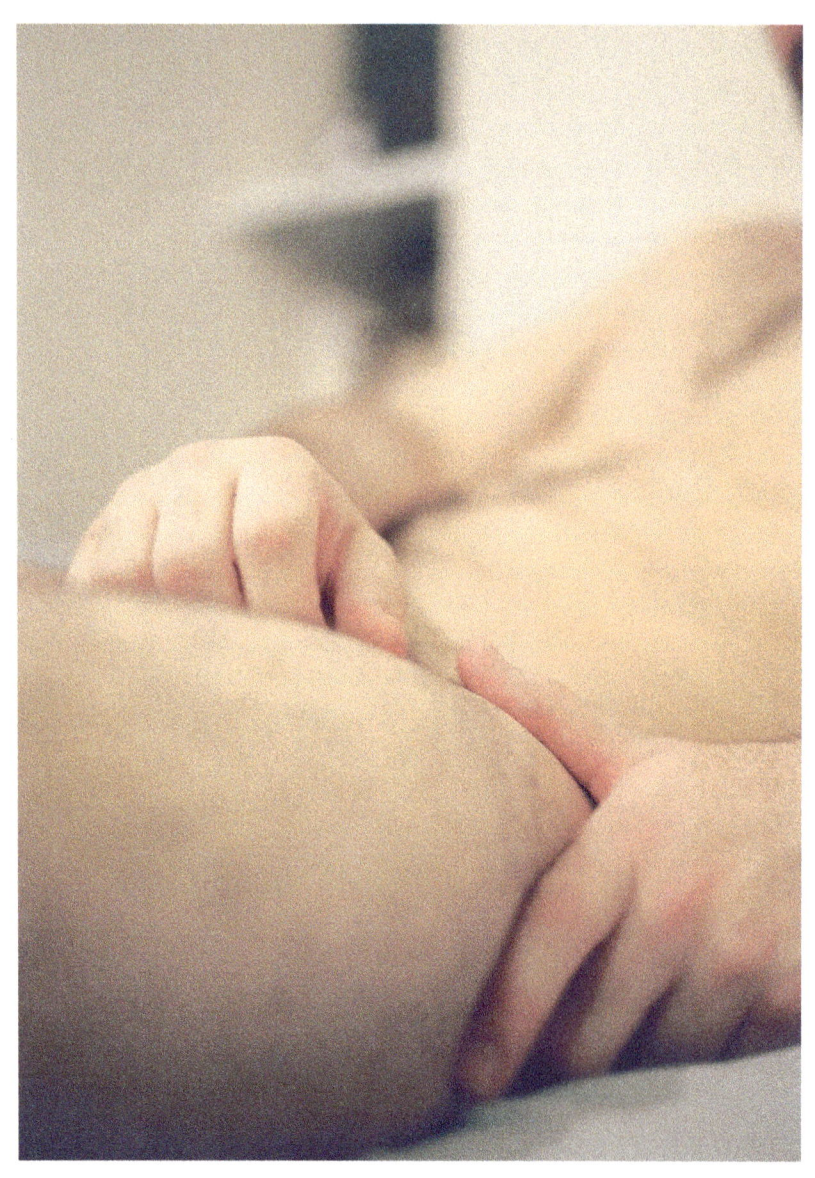

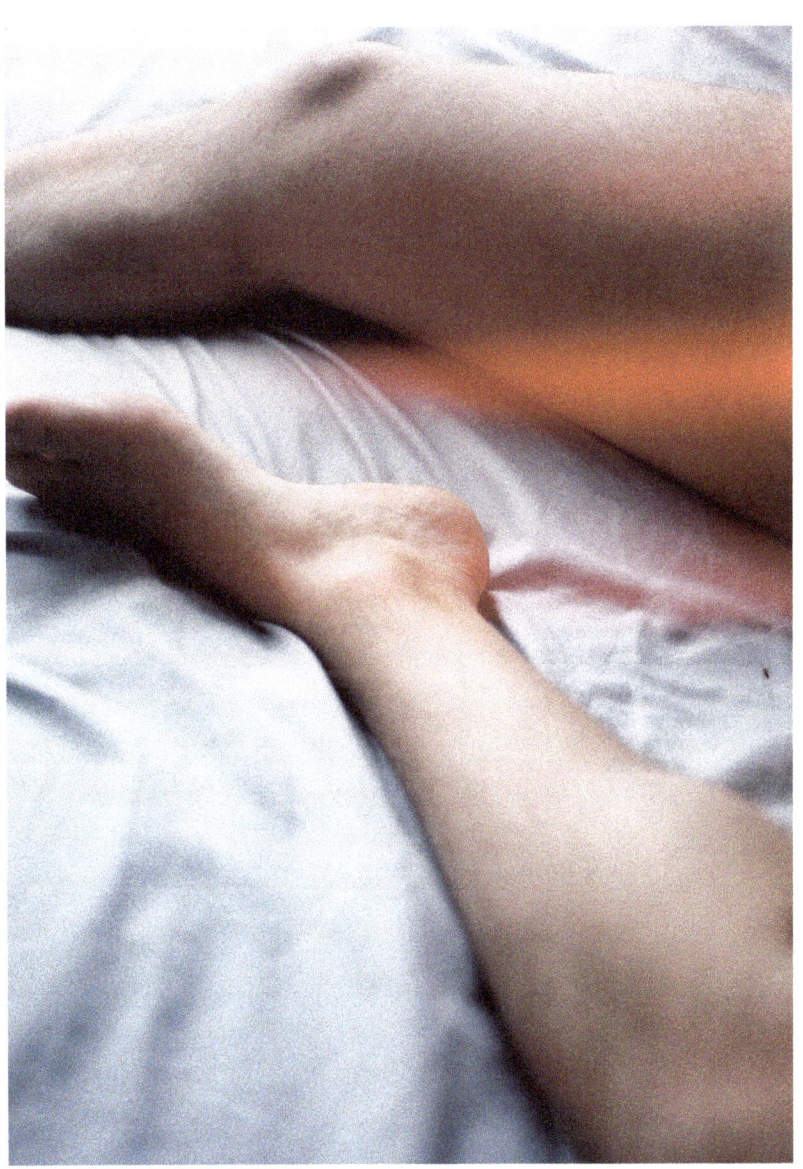

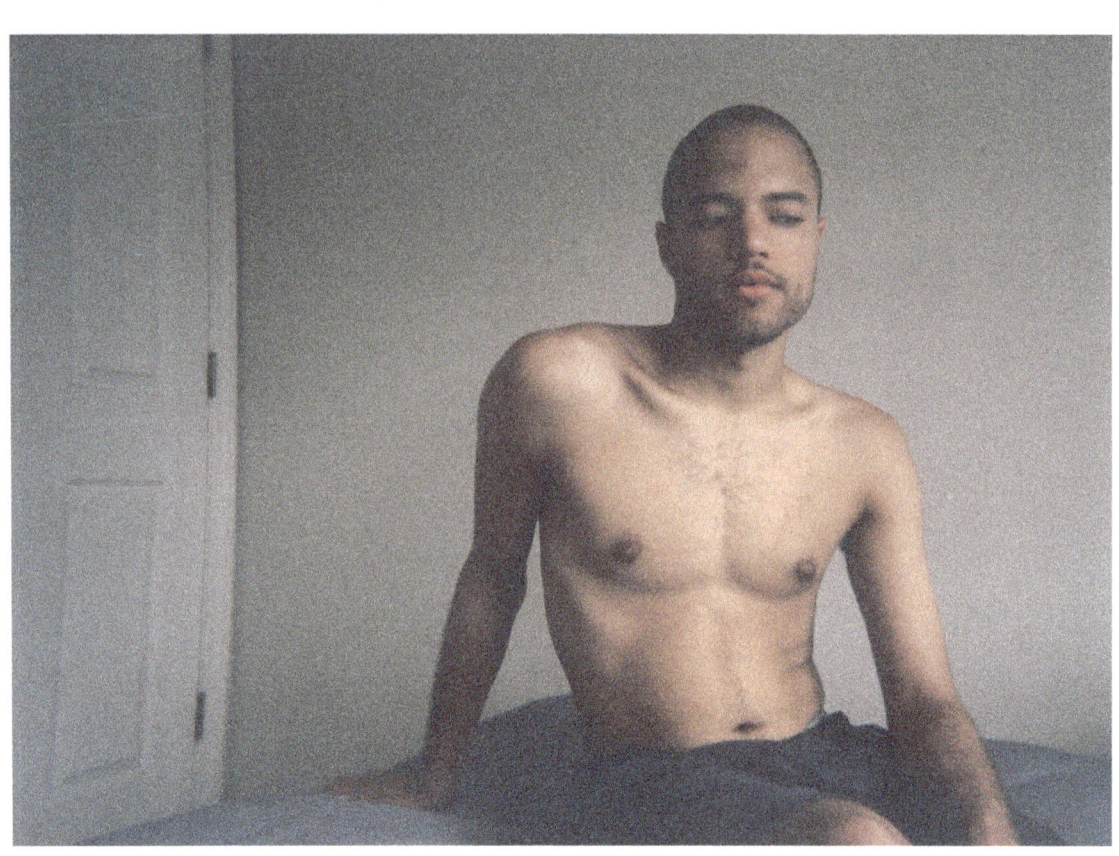

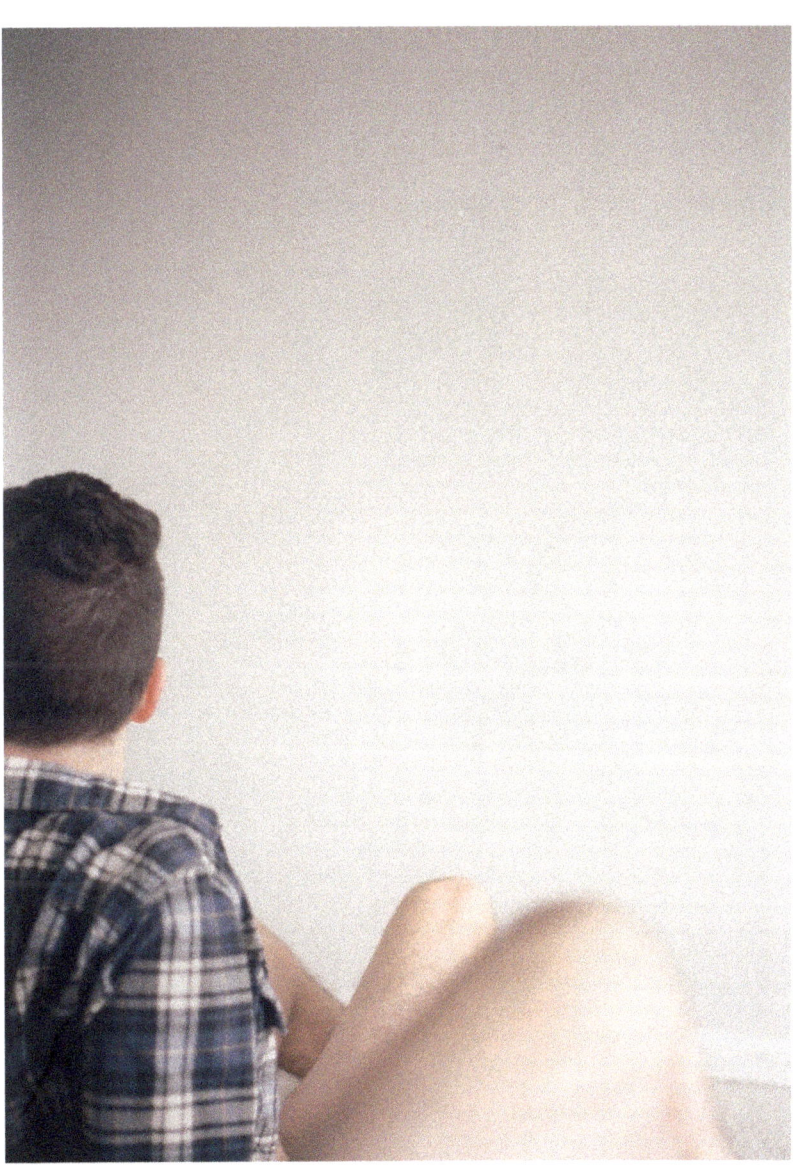

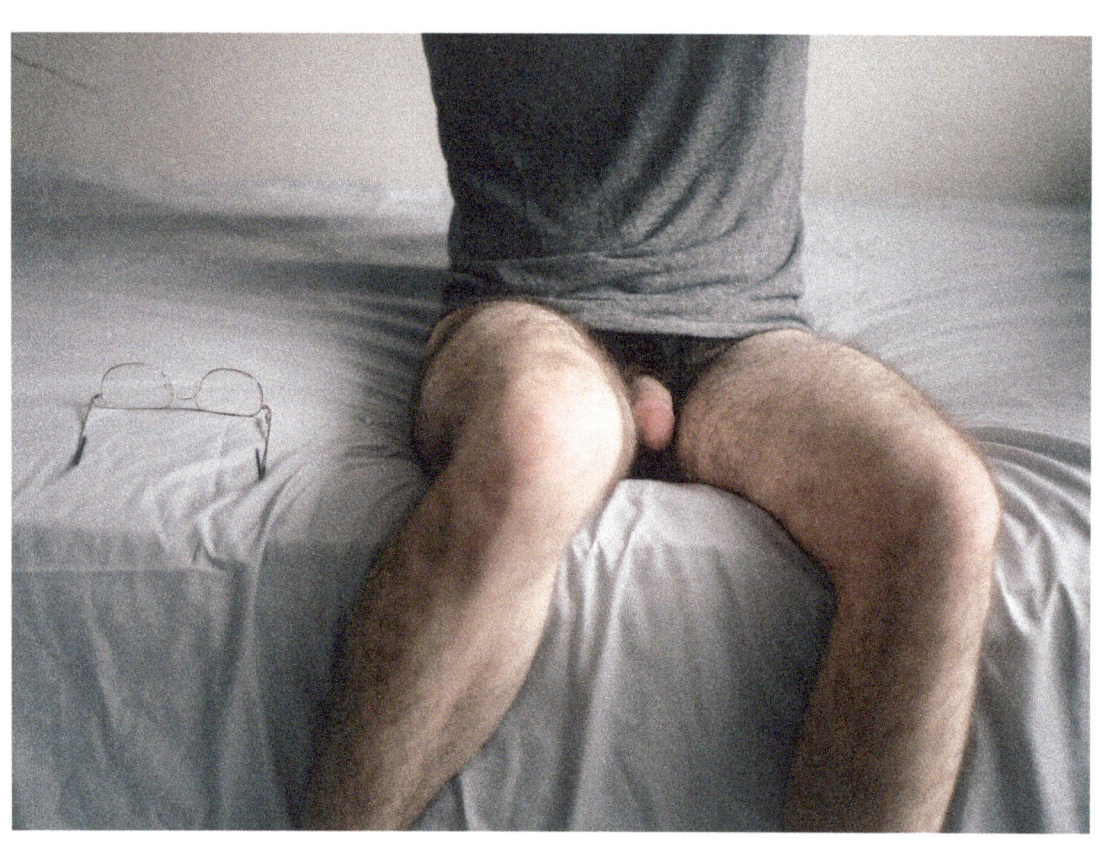

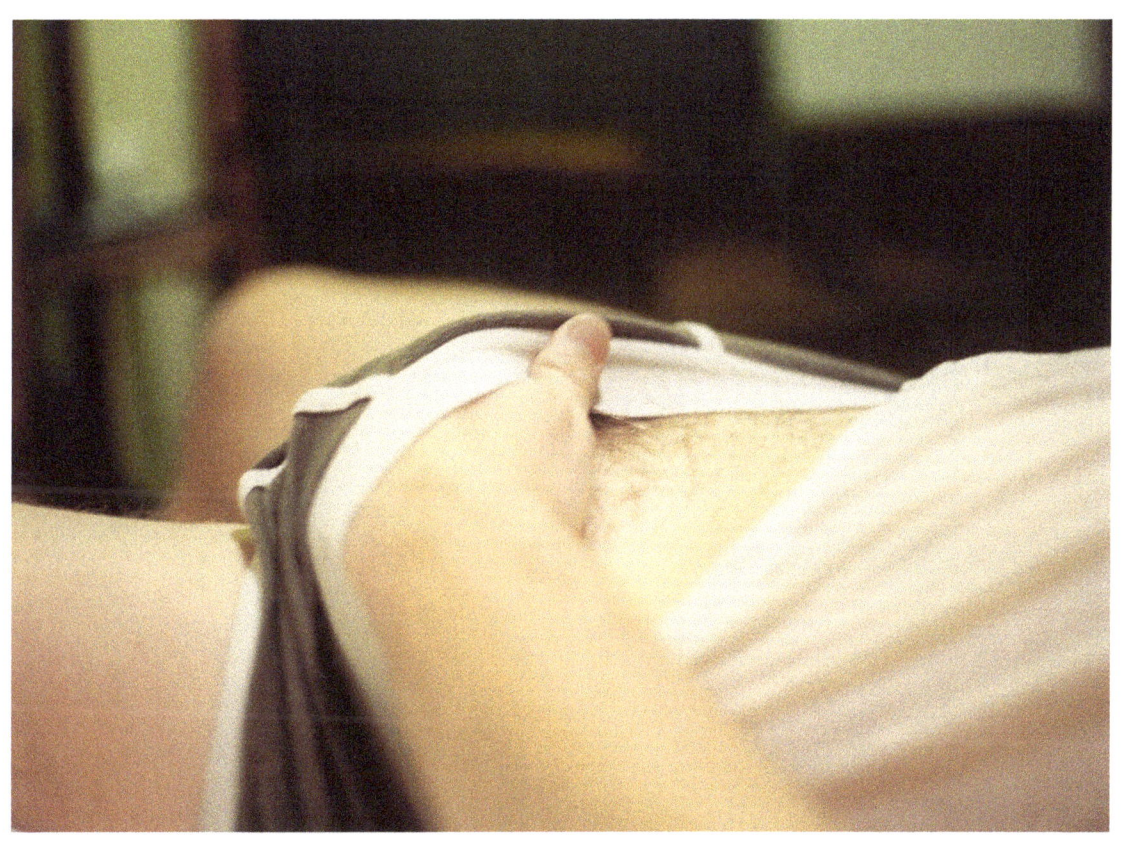

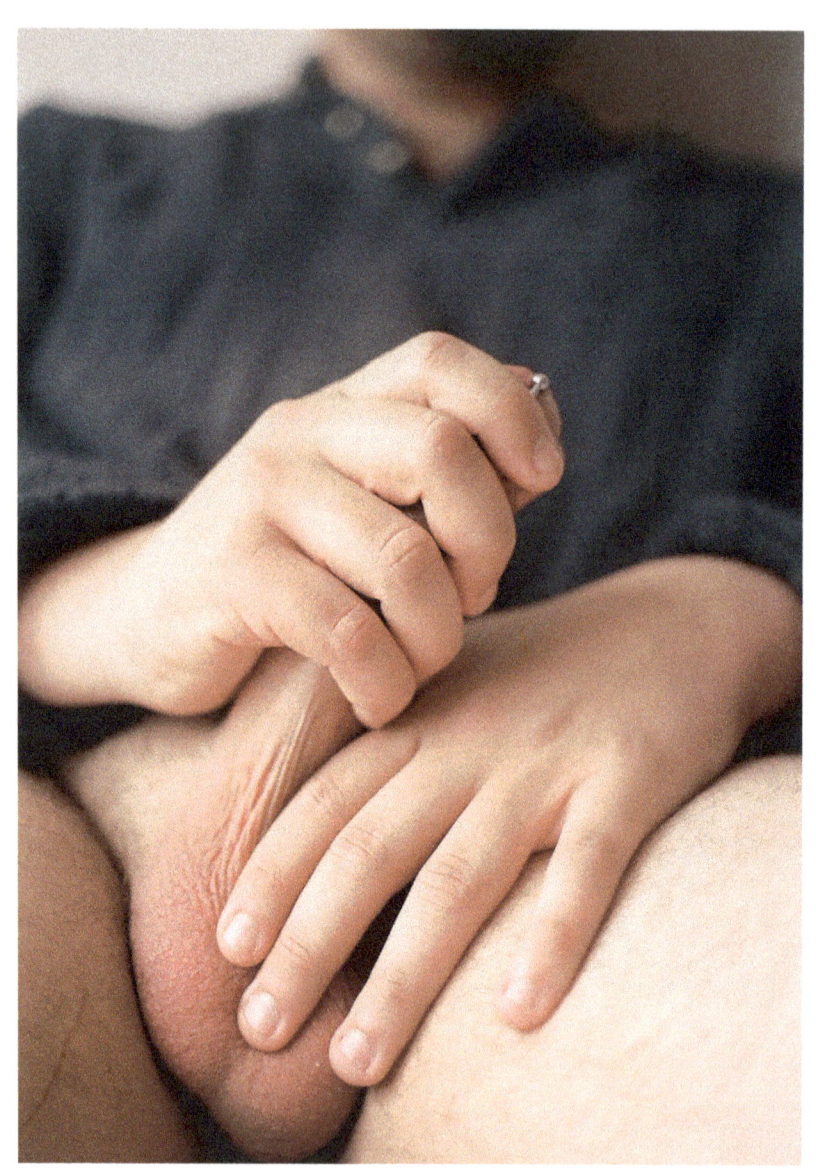

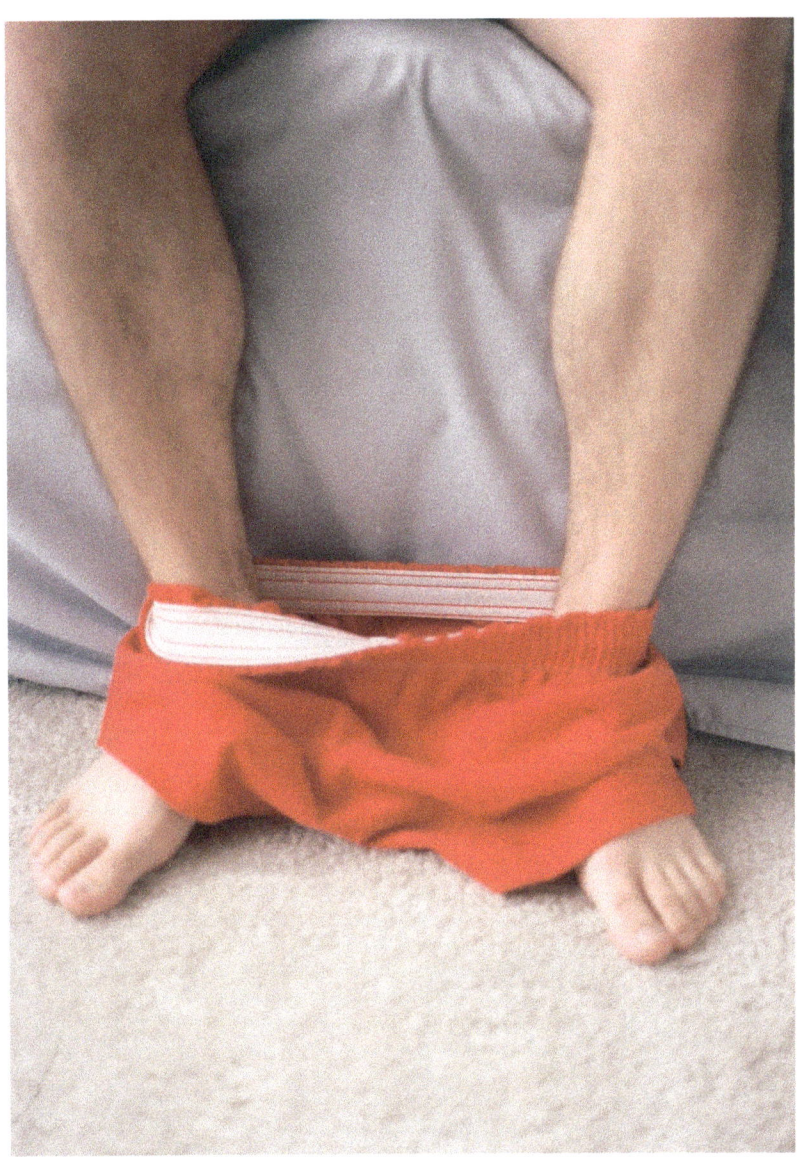

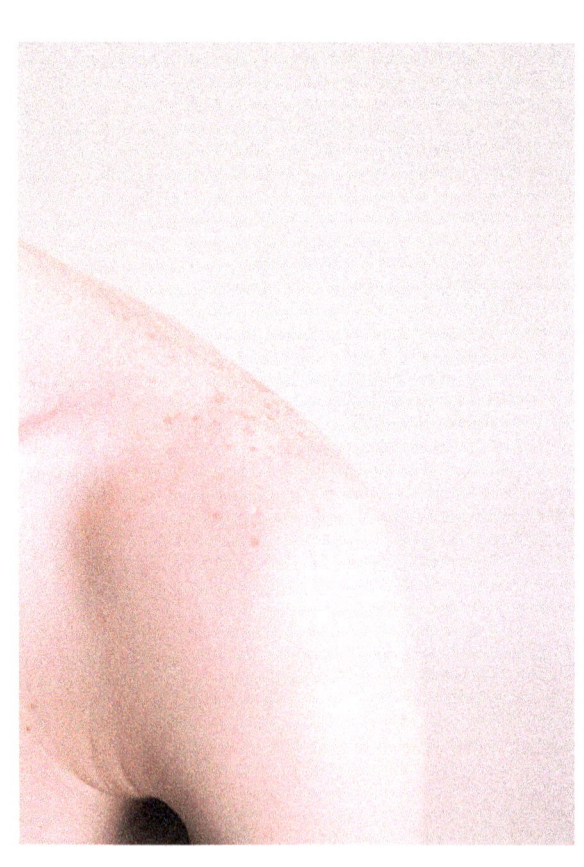

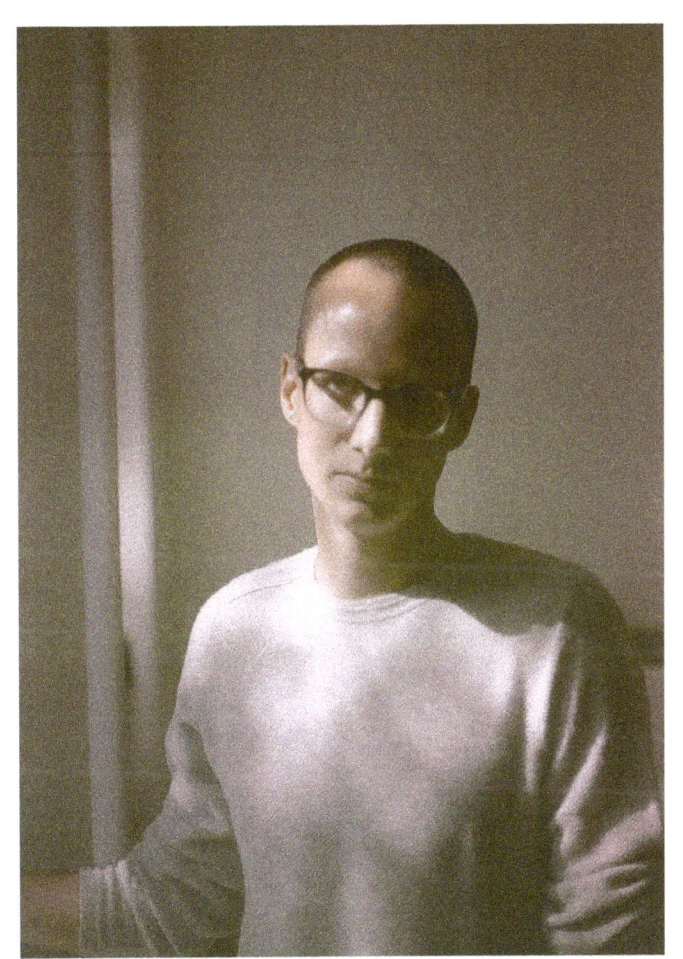

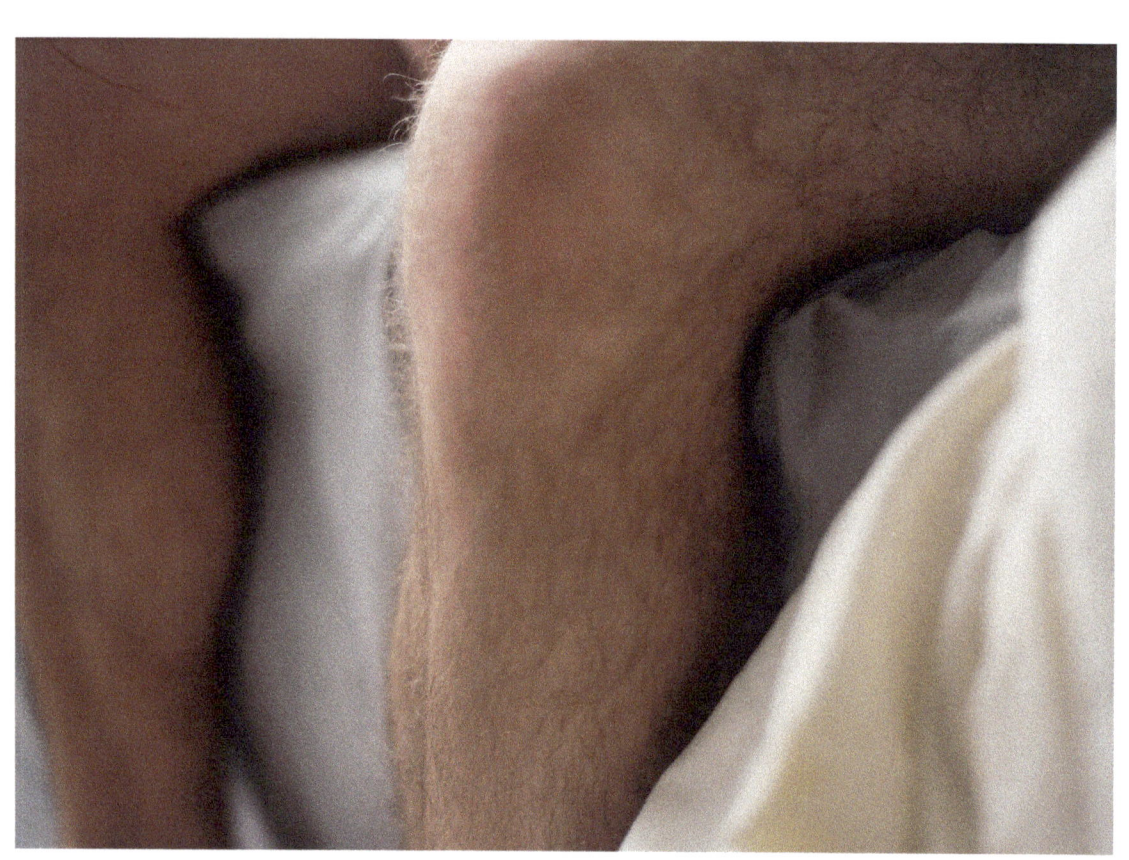

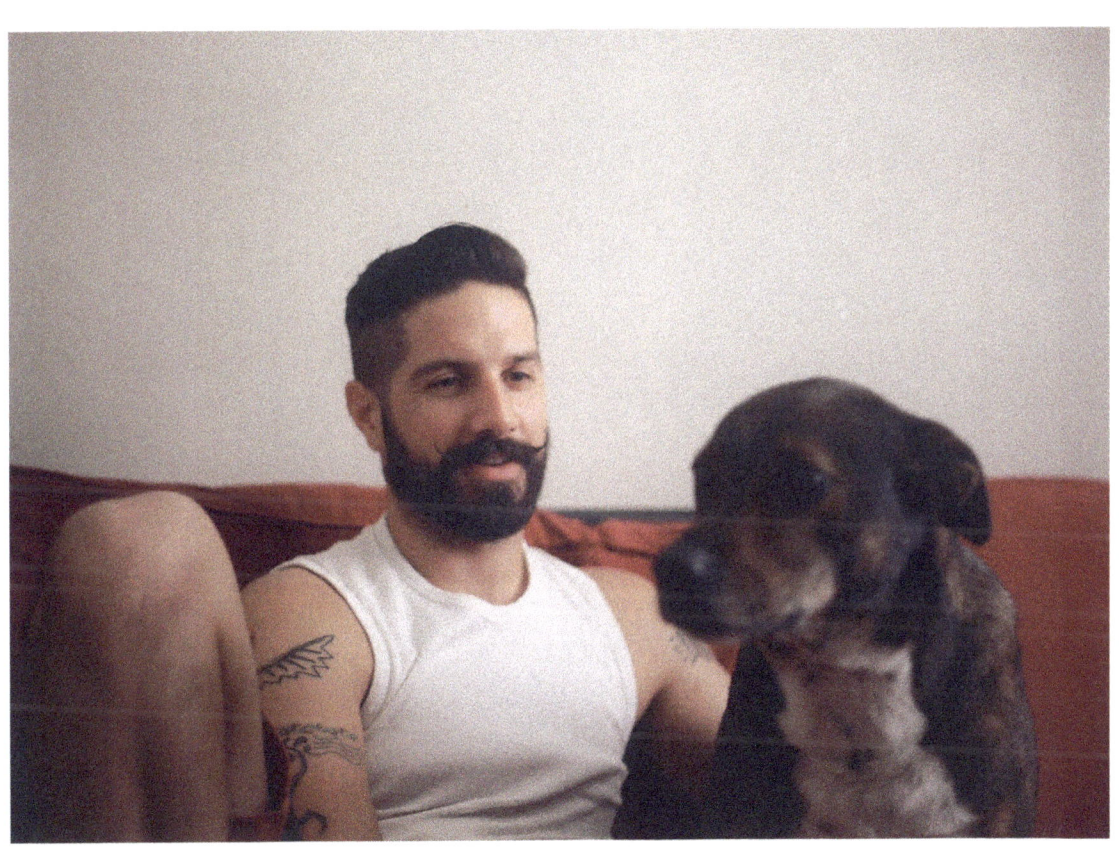

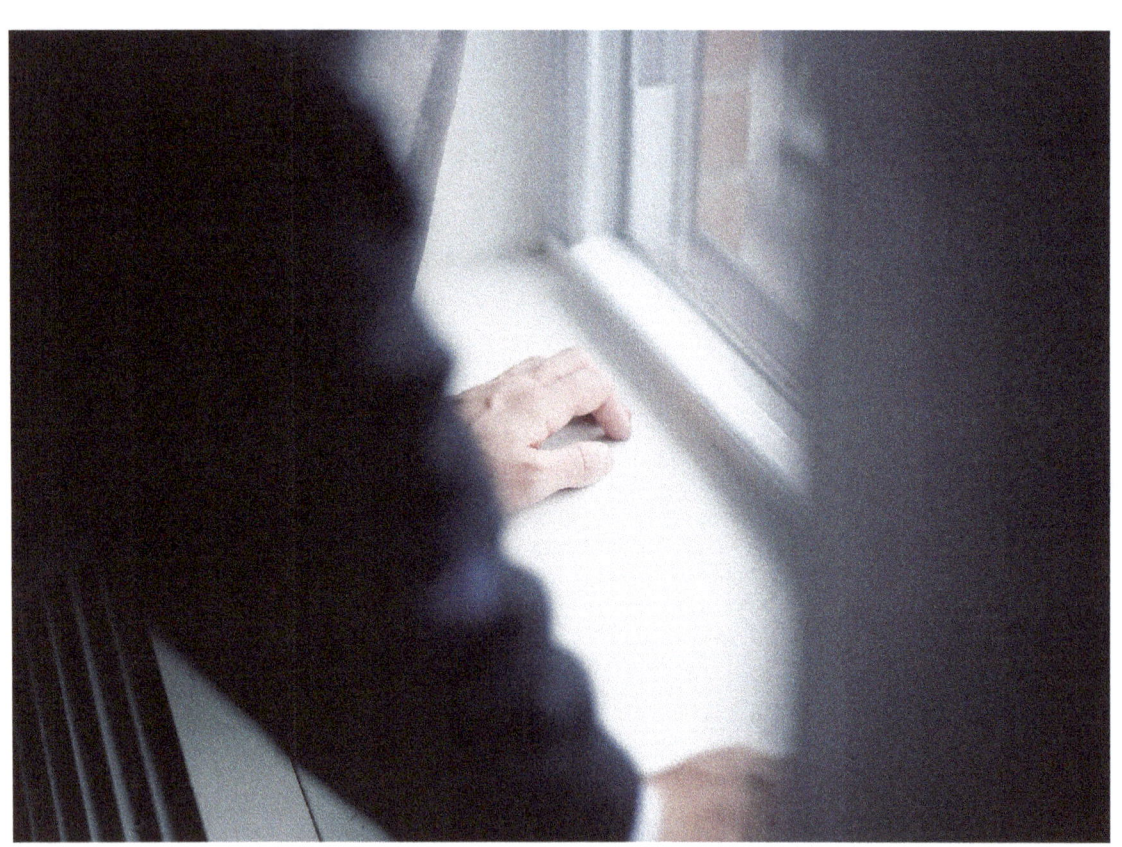

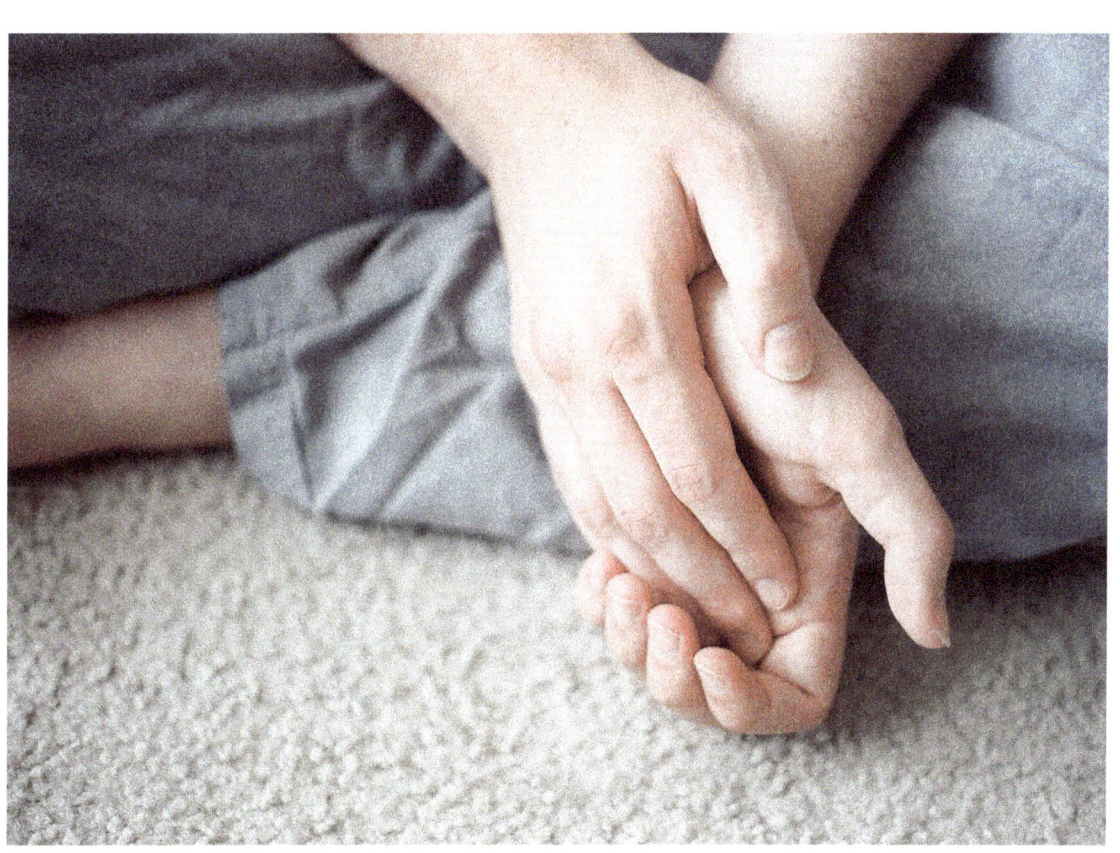

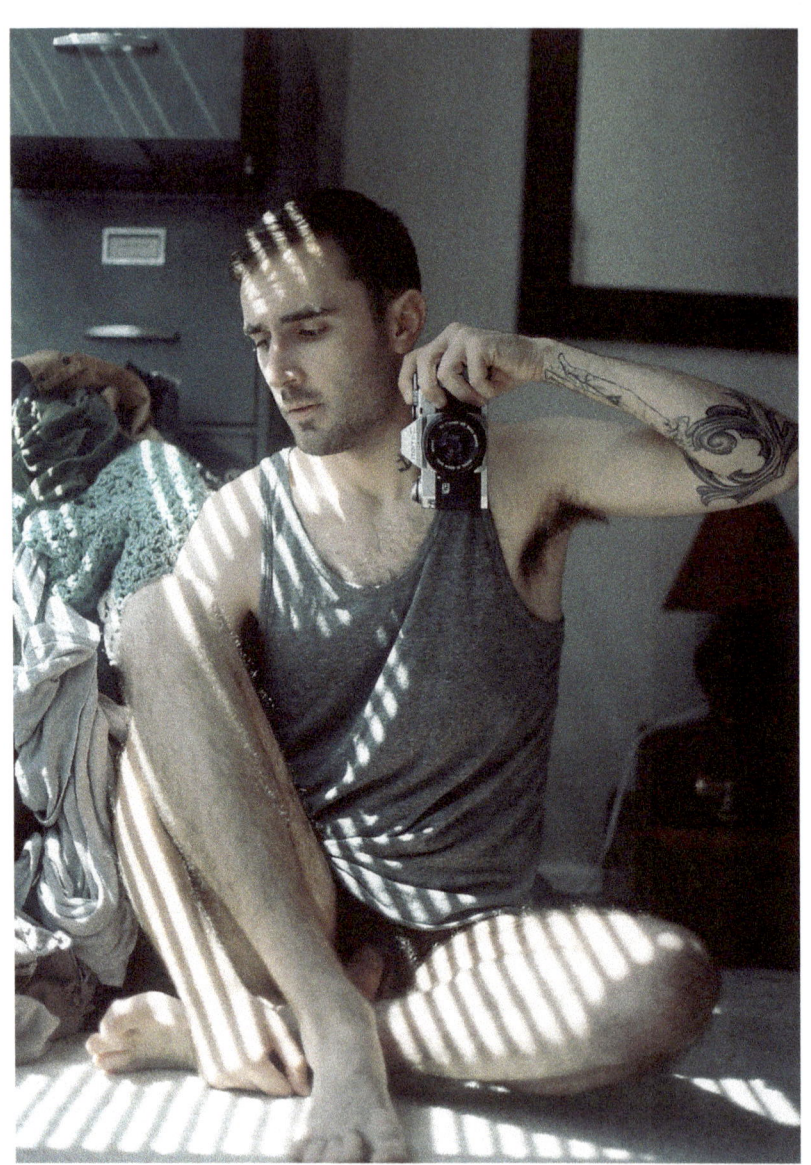

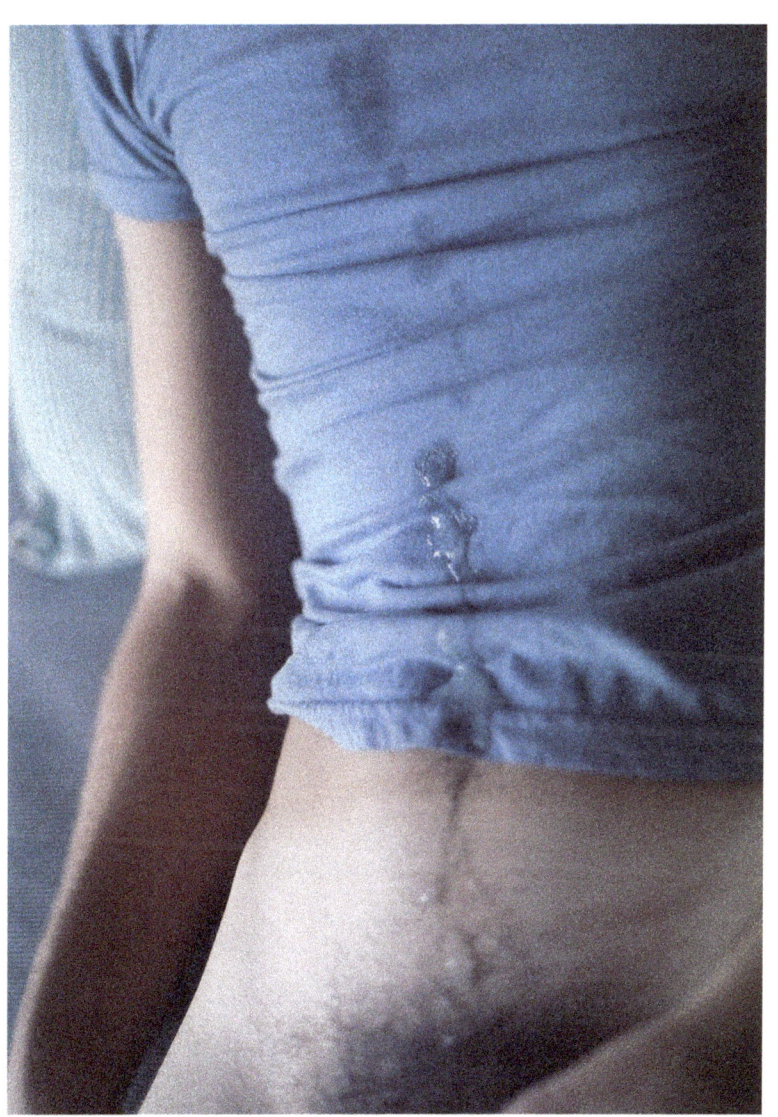

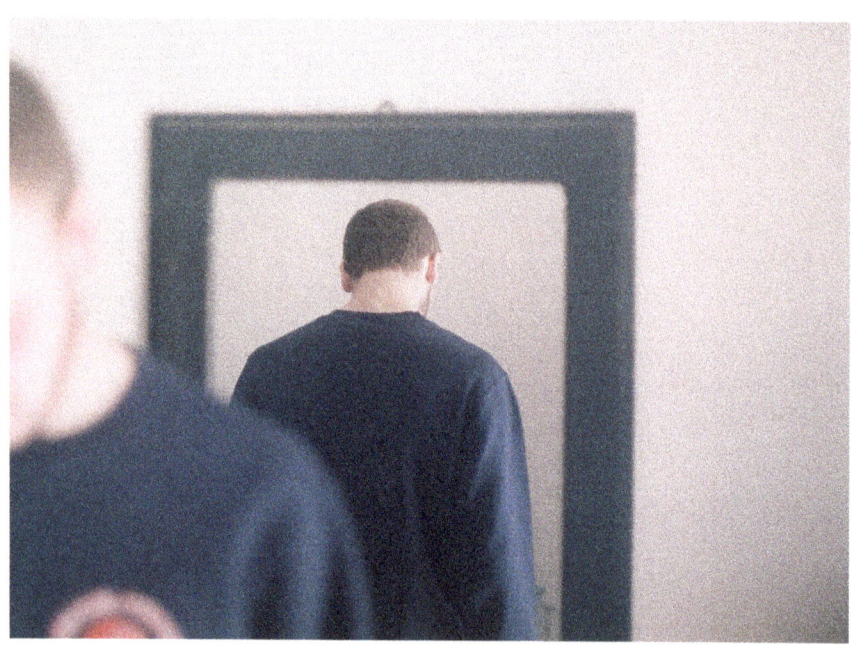

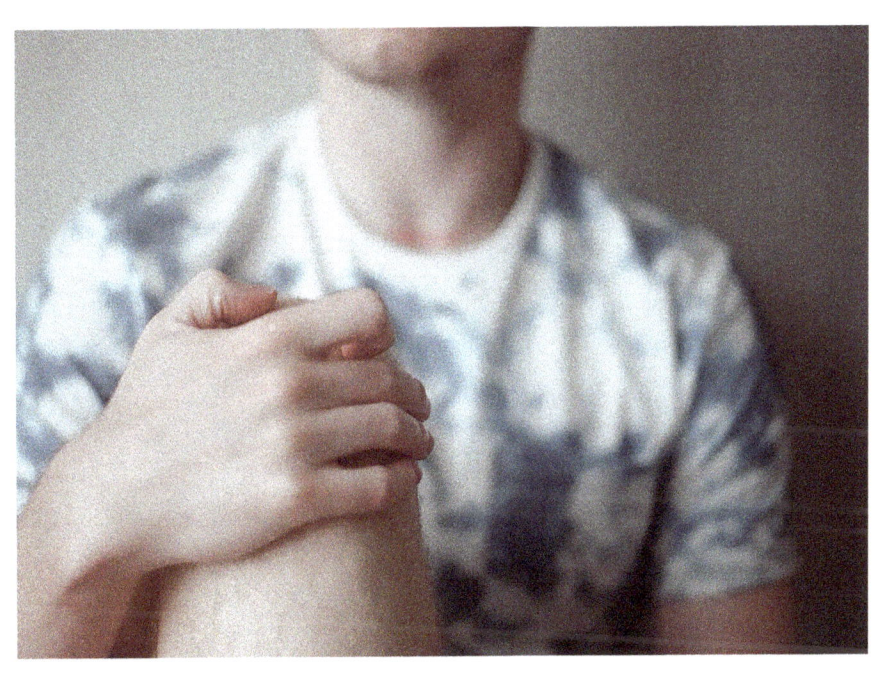

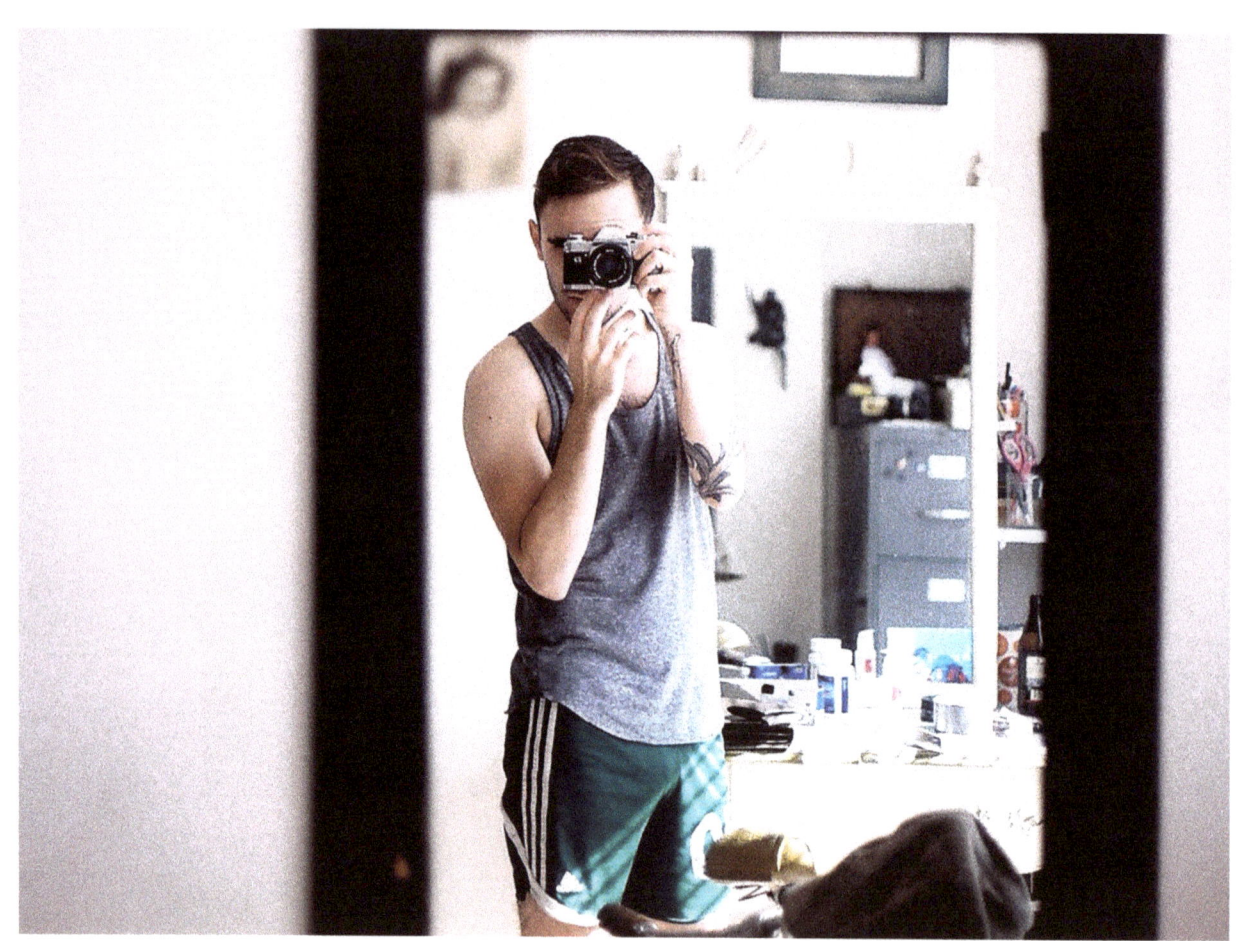

I
WILL
FOLLOW
YOU

ADAM W. CLIFTON
is a photographer living in New York City.

SIBLING RIVALRY PRESS
is an independent press based
in Little Rock, Arkansas.

www.ingramcontent.com/pod-product-compliance
Lightning Source LLC
Chambersburg PA
CBHW040547220526
45473CB00017B/3044